First World War
and Army of Occupation
War Diary
France, Belgium and Germany

36 DIVISION
Divisional Troops
Machine Gun Corps
36 Battalion
12 January 1918 - 28 February 1919

WO95/2498/3

The Naval & Military Press Ltd
www.nmarchive.com
Published in association with The National Archives

Published by

The Naval & Military Press Ltd

Unit 10 Ridgewood Industrial Park,

Uckfield, East Sussex,

TN22 5QE England

Tel: +44 (0) 1825 749494

www.naval-military-press.com

www.nmarchive.com

This diary has been reprinted in facsimile from the original. Any imperfections are inevitably reproduced and the quality may fall short of modern type and cartographic standards.

Contents

Document type	Place/Title	Date From	Date To
Heading	WO95/2498/3 36 Battalion Machine Gun Corps.		
Heading	36th Division (Divl Troops) 36th Bn Machine Gun Corps. Jan 1918-Jan 1919		
War Diary	Belton Park Grantham	12/01/1918	12/01/1918
War Diary	Southampton	13/01/1918	13/01/1918
War Diary	Le Havre	14/01/1918	16/01/1918
War Diary	Villers-St Christophe	16/01/1918	21/01/1918
War Diary	Grand Seraucourt	21/01/1918	31/01/1918
War Diary	Field	07/02/1918	28/02/1918
War Diary	Essigny In The Line	01/02/1918	01/02/1918
War Diary	In The Line	02/02/1918	28/02/1918
Heading	C. Coy 36th M.G. Battn War Diary For Month Of February, 1918		
War Diary	Happencourt	01/02/1918	15/02/1918
War Diary	In The Line	16/02/1918	28/02/1918
War Diary	Happencourt	12/02/1918	24/02/1918
War Diary	Grand Seraucourt	01/02/1918	06/02/1918
War Diary	Happencourt	07/02/1918	28/02/1918
War Diary	Grand Seraucourt	01/02/1918	07/02/1918
War Diary	Happencourt	08/02/1918	01/03/1918
Miscellaneous	Order For Relief	15/02/1918	15/02/1918
Heading	36th Divisional Troops Formed 1st March 1918 Out Of 107,108 109 & Machine Gun Companies. 36th Battalion Machine Gun Corps March 1918		
War Diary	Field	01/03/1918	20/03/1918
Miscellaneous	Programme Of Work	01/03/1918	01/03/1918
Operation(al) Order(s)	No. 36 Battalion Machine Gun Corps Order No. 1	03/03/1918	03/03/1918
Miscellaneous	36 Battn. Machine Gun Corps.	21/03/1918	21/03/1918
Miscellaneous	No. 36 Battn. Machine Gun Corps.	21/03/1918	21/03/1918
Miscellaneous	Notes On Recent Fighting As Regards Machine Guns Lessons Learnt And Suggestions.		
Diagram etc	All Positions Single Guns Except Where Otherwise Stated		
Heading	36th Divisional Machine Guns. 36th Battalion Machine Gun Corps. April 1918		
War Diary	In The Field	01/04/1918	30/04/1918
Operation(al) Order(s)	36 Battn. Machine Gun Corps Order No. 3	06/04/1918	06/04/1918
Operation(al) Order(s)	36th Battalion Machine Gun Corps Order No. 4	08/04/1918	08/04/1918
Operation(al) Order(s)	36 Battalion Machine Gun Corps Order No. 6	10/04/1918	10/04/1918
Operation(al) Order(s)	36 Battalion Machine Gun Corps Order No. 7	12/04/1918	12/04/1918
Operation(al) Order(s)	No 36 Battalion Machine Gun Corps Order No. 8	15/04/1918	15/04/1918
Operation(al) Order(s)	No 36 Battalion Machine Gun Corps Order No. 9	17/04/1918	17/04/1918
Operation(al) Order(s)	No 36 Battalion Machine Gun Corps Order No. 10	20/04/1918	20/04/1918
Miscellaneous	No 36 Battalion Machine Gun Corps	21/04/1918	21/04/1918
Operation(al) Order(s)	No 36 Battalion Machine Gun Corps Order No. 11	22/04/1918	22/04/1918
Operation(al) Order(s)	No 36 Battalion Machine Gun Corps Order No. 12	25/04/1918	25/04/1918
Operation(al) Order(s)	No 36 Battalion Machine Gun Corps Order No. 13	28/04/1918	28/04/1918
War Diary		01/05/1918	31/05/1918
Operation(al) Order(s)	No 36 Battalion Machine Gun Corps Order No. 14	04/05/1918	04/05/1918
Operation(al) Order(s)	No 36 Battalion Machine Gun Corps Order No. 15	10/05/1918	10/05/1918

Operation(al) Order(s)	No 36 Battalion Machine Gun Corps Order No. 16	13/05/1918	13/05/1918
Operation(al) Order(s)	No 36 Battn Machine Gun Corps Order No. 17	21/05/1918	21/05/1918
War Diary		01/06/1918	29/06/1918
War Diary	Field	30/06/1918	30/06/1918
War Diary	On Service.	01/07/1918	31/07/1918
Operation(al) Order(s)	No 36 Battalion Machine Gun Corps Order No. 21	06/07/1918	06/07/1918
Operation(al) Order(s)	No 36 Battalion Machine Gun Corps Order No 20	02/07/1918	02/07/1918
War Diary	In The Field	01/08/1918	31/08/1918
War Diary	On Service	01/09/1918	30/09/1918
Diagram etc	Identification Trace for use with Artillery Maps.		
Operation(al) Order(s)	No 36 Battalion Machine Gun Corps Order No. 42	08/09/1918	08/09/1918
Operation(al) Order(s)	36th Battalion Machine Gun Corps Order No 41	07/09/1918	07/09/1918
Operation(al) Order(s)	No 36 Battalion Machine Gun Corps Order No 42.A	16/09/1918	16/09/1918
War Diary	On Service.	01/10/1918	27/11/1918
War Diary	In The Field	00/12/1918	31/01/1919
War Diary	Mourucourt	01/02/1919	28/02/1919

WO95/2498/3

36 Battalion Machine Gun Corps.

36TH DIVISION
(DIVL TROOPS)

36TH BN MACHINE GUN CORPS.

JAN 1918 - JAN 1919

Army Form C. 2[illegible]8.

Instructions regarding War Diaries and Intelligence Summaries are contained in F. S. Regs., Part II. and the Staff Manual respectively. Title pages will be prepared in manuscript.

WAR DIARY
or
INTELLIGENCE SUMMARY.
(*Erase heading not required.*)

266 Machine Gun Corps

Vol I

Place	Date	Hour	Summary of Events and Information	Remarks and references to Appendices
Belton Park Grantham	12/1/18	7.30 Pm	Left for Port of Embarkation SOUTHAMPTON.	
SOUTHAMPTON	13/1/18	7.30 Am	Arrived SOUTHAMPTON DOCKS - Remained in Docks all day	36th Bn MGC
SOUTHAMPTON	13/1/18	6 PM	Embarked for LE HAVRE	Jan '18
LE HAVRE	14/1/18	9 AM	Landed at LE HAVRE - Proceeded to No 2 Rest Camp	Jan '19
LE HAVRE	15/1/18		No 2 Rest Camp	
LE HAVRE	16/1/18	9 PM	Entrained at LA GARE DES MARCHANDISES for VILLERS - ST - CHRISTOPHE	
VILLERS-ST CHRISTOPHE	17/1/18	2.30 Pm	Detrained at VILLERS. - ST - CHRISTOPHE - Company billeted in Huts	
VILLERS-ST CHRISTOPHE	18/1/18		In billets at VILLERS - ST - CHRISTOPHE.	
VILLERS-ST CHRISTOPHE	19/1/18		In billets at VILLERS - ST - CHRISTOPHE	
VILLERS - ST-CHRISTOPHE	20/1/18		In billets at VILLERS - ST - CHRISTOPHE.	
VILLERS-ST CHRISTOPHE	21/1/18	1 Pm	Proceeded by route march to GRAND SERAUCOURT.	
GRAND SÉRAUCOURT	21/1/18	4 Pm	Arrived at GRAND SÉRAUCOURT ~~4 Pm~~ Company in Huts	

A7092). Wt. W12839/M1293 750,000. 1/17. D. D & L. Ltd. Forms/C2118/14.

Instructions regarding War Diaries and Intelligence Summaries are contained in F. S. Regs., Part II. and the Staff Manual respectively. Title pages will be prepared in manuscript.

WAR DIARY
or
INTELLIGENCE SUMMARY.
(Erase heading not required.)

Army Form C. 2118.

Place	Date	Hour	Summary of Events and Information	Remarks and references to Appendices
GRAND-SÉRAUCOURT	22/1/18		In Huts at GRAND SÉRAUCOURT.	
GRAND SÉRAUCOURT	23/1/18		In Huts at GRAND SÉRAUCOURT	
GRAND SÉRAUCOURT	24/1/18		In Huts at GRAND SÉRAUCOURT	
GRAND SÉRAUCOURT	25/1/18		In Huts at GRAND SÉRAUCOURT	
GRAND SÉRAUCOURT	26/1/18		In Huts at GRAND SÉRAUCOURT	
GRAND SÉRAUCOURT	27/1/18		–do– Half company occupied reserve gun positions.	
GRAND SÉRAUCOURT	28/1/18		— do —	
GRAND SÉRAUCOURT	29/1/18		— do —	
GRAND SÉRAUCOURT	30/1/18		— do —	
GRAND SÉRAUCOURT	31/1/18		— do —	

A7092. Wt. W12839/M1293 750,000. 1/17. D. D & L. Ltd. Forms/C2118/14.

Army Form C. 2118.

Instructions regarding War Diaries and Intelligence Summaries are contained in F. S. Regs., Part II. and the Staff Manual respectively. Title pages will be prepared in manuscript.

WAR DIARY
or
INTELLIGENCE SUMMARY.
(*Erase heading not required.*)

Place	Date	Hour	Summary of Events and Information	Remarks and references to Appendices
Field	7/2/18	LSB	Quiet period we fired 13,000 rounds during the evening.	
	8/2/18	LSB	Quiet period few shells on CAUCHY [illegible] day & no aerial activity	
			5,000 rounds fired particular attention paid to movement in	
			the RUCOURT SALIENT Capt [illegible] joined	
	9/2/18	LSB	Quiet period. we fired 5,000 rounds at night.	
	10/2/18	LSB	Artillery still quiet, but enemy machine guns more active, we retaliated	
			by firing 6,547 rounds during the night.	
	11/2/18	LSB.	Artillery rather more active, enemy shells fell near No 10 guns, a direct hit	
			being scored in FAVEL ALLEY. Enemy bombing planes were again over	
			our lines, we fired 4,000 rounds during the evening & early part	
			of the night.	
	12/2/18	LSB	Period quiet, we fired 6,000 rounds during the night.	
	13/2/18	LSB.	Our Artillery was more active though the enemy's was very inactive	
			Enemy machine guns less active, we fired 4000 rounds	
	14/2/18	LSB.	Again quiet. practically no artillery fire owing to poor observation	
			Our guns fired 5000 rounds during the night.	

D. D. & L., London, E.C.
(A7883) Wt W809/M1672 350,000 4/17 Sch 52a Forms/C/2118/14

Army Form C. 2118.

WAR DIARY
or
INTELLIGENCE SUMMARY.
(Erase heading not required.)

Instructions regarding War Diaries and Intelligence Summaries are contained in F. S. Regs., Part II, and the Staff Manual respectively. Title pages will be prepared in manuscript.

Place	Date	Hour	Summary of Events and Information	Remarks and references to Appendices
[illegible]ula	15/2/18	[illegible]	Period quiet, usual night firing carried on. No 12 position changed	
"	16/2/18	[illegible]	Day quiet. Relieved by 10[illegible] Company. Company went to	
			HAPPENCOURT.	
	17/2/18		Training company. Gun drill etc. Programme attached	
	18/2			
	19/2			
	20/2			
	21/2			
	22/2	[illegible]	19 Attached men formed.	
	23/2		Training under 266 Coy.	
	24/2		carried on.	
	24/2		14 Guns went into line. O.O. attached.	
	25/2	[illegible]	Period quiet. Headquarters at HAPPENCOURT. HAMEL Rock Shelter	
	26/2	[illegible]	Slight increase in activity. Aircraft very active. No night fighting	
	27/2	[illegible]	Trench mortars active. Enemy attempted raid but was repulsed leaving	
			one dead.	

D. D. & L., London, E.C.
(A7883) Wt W8c9/M1672 350,000 4/17 Sch 52a Forms/C/2118/14

Instructions regarding War Diaries and Intelligence Summaries are contained in F. S. Regs., Part II. and the Staff Manual respectively. Title pages will be prepared in manuscript.

WAR DIARY
or
INTELLIGENCE SUMMARY.
(Erase heading not required.)

Army Form C. 2118.

Place	Date	Hour	Summary of Events and Information	Remarks and references to Appendices
Field	28/2/18	BB	Day quiet Standing to in afternoon, and reinforcing Battle Zone night quiet also.	

D. D. & L., London, E.C.
(A7883) Wt W809/M1672 350,000 4/17 Sch. 52a Forms/C/2118/14

Army Form C. 2118.

B Coy
36th MG Batt

WAR DIARY
or
INTELLIGENCE SUMMARY.
(Erase heading not required.)

Instructions regarding War Diaries and Intelligence Summaries are contained in F. S. Regs., Part II. and the Staff Manual respectively. Title pages will be prepared in manuscript.

Place	Date	Hour	Summary of Events and Information	Remarks and references to Appendices
ESSIGNY			REF MAP { FRANCE 66c. N.W. 1:20,000	
IN THE LINE	1st Feb		Weather:- Heavy Frost + Mist all day	
			M3 M7 M8 M9 Guns laid on S.O.S. positions — did not fire	
			M1 GOZET M11 Guns mounted throughout the night only — did not fire	S.A.B.
			INTELLIGENCE NIL CASUALTIES NIL	
IN THE LINE	2nd		Weather:- Heavy Frost in early morning. Fine day with sunshine	
			M3 M7 M8 M9 laid on S.O.S lines. Between 6.30 + midnight M7 fired 1250 rounds at Target	
			B10 a 55.20 to B10 b 45.70. Number 3 gun of M8 fired 1750 rounds at B 8 b. 31.40 to B 8 d 75.05.	
			M1 GOZET M11 Guns ~~laid on direct target~~ mounted for direct fire. Between 6.30 pm + 12 midnight	
			M11 fired 1250 rounds at cross roads B 10 a 32.25.	
			Total rounds fired 4250	
			INTELLIGENCE NIL CASUALTIES NIL	S.A.B.
IN THE LINE	3rd		Weather:- Fine with Sunshine. Night firing carried out as follows:-	
			M7 guns fired 1500 rounds on B 3 d 60.28. – B 4 c 18.86. Intermittent bursts from 7.30 pm. to MIDNIGHT	
			M8 guns fired 1500 rounds from M3 position on B 3 b 80.02 to B 3 b 80.65. intermittently from	
			midnight to dawn. M3 M9 Guns laid on S.O.S. lines — did not fire	
			M1 GOZET M11 Guns mounted for direct fire – did not fire	

D. D. & L., London, E.C.
(A7883) Wt W809/M1672 350,000 4/17 Sch. 52a Forms/C/2118/14

Instructions regarding War Diaries and Intelligence Summaries are contained in F. S. Regs., Part II. and the Staff Manual respectively. Title pages will be prepared in manuscript.

WAR DIARY
or
INTELLIGENCE SUMMARY.
(Erase heading not required.)

Army Form C. 2118.

Place	Date	Hour	Summary of Events and Information	Remarks and references to Appendices
	3rd (continued)		INTELLIGENCE NIL CASUALTIES 1 O.R. wounded at M3 position but remained on duty.	
			RELIEF by SECTIONS carried out:- No.1. Section relieved No.4 + took over position M7 + GOZET in LEFT GROUP. No.4 Section relieved No.2. Section + took over positions M1 + M3 in RIGHT GROUP. No.2 Section relieved No.3 Section + took over M8 positions in RIGHT GROUP No.3 Section occupied position M9 + M11 in RESERVE GROUP.	
			RELIEF Carried out without incident.	SWH.
In THE LINE	4th		Weather Fine with Sunshine. Owing to wiring being done in front of gun positions during night, there was no Night firing.	
			M1 GOZET M11 mounted for direct fire. Did not fire.	
			M3 M7 M8 M9 laid on S.O.S. lines — did not fire	
			One gun taken from M11 position for repair. 15 guns only in the line	
			INTELLIGENCE:- Scattered shelling between GOZET + ESSIGNY — ST. QUENTIN road between 2 + 3 pm. NO DAMAGE. 4·2 + 5·9 calibre, 20-30 shells.	
			CASUALTIES NIL	SWH.
In THE LINE	5th		Weather FINE with Sunshine. Night firing as follows:-	
			M7 gun fired 1500 rds. at target B10 a 55.20 to road B10 b 45.70 between 9 pm + 3 am.	

D. D. & L., London, E.C. (A7883) Wt W809/M1672 550,000 4/17 Sch. 52a. Forms/C/2118/14

Instructions regarding War Diaries and Intelligence Summaries are contained in F. S. Regs., Part II. and the Staff Manual respectively. Title pages will be prepared in manuscript.

WAR DIARY
or
INTELLIGENCE SUMMARY.
(Erase heading not required.)

Army Form C. 2118.

Place	Date	Hour	Summary of Events and Information	Remarks and references to Appendices
	5th (Continued)		M8 gun (No. 3) fired 1500 rds. at B3 b 80.02 to B5 b 90.65.	
			M11 fired 1000 rounds at Cross roads B10 a 32.25.	
			M1 & GOZET laid for direct fire. Did not fire	
			M3 & M9 guns laid on S.O.S. lines – did not fire	
			INTELLIGENCE – NIL CASUALTIES NIL	S.W.H.
IN THE LINE	6th		Weather:- Dull Night firing carried out as follows:-	
			M4 position 1500 rounds fired at B3 c 5.0. to B9 b 5.7. between 6 pm. & midnight	
			M8 position 1500 rounds fired at B3 b 80.02. to B3 b 90.65. from 6 pm. 6th to 6 a.m. (7th)	
			M11 position 1000 rounds fired at Cross roads B10 a. 32.25.	
			Intelligence NIL Casualties NIL	S.W.H.
IN the LINE	7th		Weather wet & dull. The following night firing was carried out:- M4 position 1500 rounds fired between 6 pm. & midnight at a target B9 b 50.70 to B10 a 20.80. From M8 position 1500 rounds were fired at B8 b 31.40 to B1 d 75.05	
			Intelligence NIL Casualties NIL	S.W.H.
IN the LINE	8th		Weather wet & high wind. Night firing as follows:- M8 fired 1000 rounds at B3 b 90.40 from 6 p. to ~~5 pm~~ ~~8~~ 8 pm.	

(over

D. D. & L., London, E.C. (A7883) Wt. W809/M1672 350,000 4/17 Sch. 52a Forms/C/2118/14

Instructions regarding War Diaries and Intelligence Summaries are contained in F. S. Regs., Part II. and the Staff Manual respectively. Title pages will be prepared in manuscript.

WAR DIARY
or
INTELLIGENCE SUMMARY.
(*Erase heading not required.*)

Army Form C. 2118.

Place	Date	Hour	Summary of Events and Information	Remarks and references to Appendices
	8th continued		M7 fired 1000 rounds at B3d 62.51 between 8 pm. 8th + 4 a.m. 9th.	
			Intelligence Nil Casualties NIL.	S.W.
In the LINE	9th		Weather Fine sunshine High Wind.	
			Night Firing:- M8 fired 2000 rounds at B10 b 88.82 to B5c 54.31. between 6 pm + midnight	
			M9 (alternative emplacement) fired 2000 rounds between 6 p. 9th + 6 a.m. 10th at B8 b 40.17	
			Intelligence NIL Casualties 1 O.R. Shrapnel wound in left forearm at M3 position	S.W.
In the Line	10th		Weather Fine. High Wind.	
			NIGHT FIRING:- M8 position 2000 rounds were fired between 6 pm + 11 pm. at B3 b 90.35 to	
			B4c 09.50. – M9 position. 1500 rounds fired at Trenches B9a 00.50 to B9b 50.70.–	
			M7 position. Between 9 pm. + 3. a.m. (11th) 1500 rounds fired at Trenches B3c 50.00 to	
			B9b 50.70. 71 GOZET M11 laid for direct fire – did not fire.	
			M3 laid on S.O.S. lines – did not fire.	
			Intelligence NIL Casualties NIL	S.W.
In the Line	11th		Weather FINE	
			Night Firing from M7 position 1000 rounds at B9b 5.7. to B10.a. 2.8. between 9 pm. +	
			3. a.m.	

D. D. & L., London, E.C.
(A7883) Wt. W809/M1672 350,000 4/17 Sch. 52a Forms/C/2118/14

Army Form C. 2118.

Instructions regarding War Diaries and Intelligence Summaries are contained in F. S. Regs., Part II. and the Staff Manual respectively. Title pages will be prepared in manuscript.

WAR DIARY
or
INTELLIGENCE SUMMARY.
(*Erase heading not required.*)

Place	Date	Hour	Summary of Events and Information	Remarks and references to Appendices
	11th continued		M1 GOZET M11 mounted for direct fire – did not fire	
			M8 M3 M9 Guns laid on S.O.S. line – did not fire	
			Intelligence NIL Casualties NIL	S.W.K.
In the LINE	12th		Weather FINE with sunshine. The following NIGHT FIRING was carried out:–	
			M7 position 1000 rounds fired between 8 pm + 2 am. at Trenches B3c 5.0 to B9b 5.7.	
			M9 position between midnight and 4. am. 1000 rounds fired at Trenches B9a 00.50 – B9.a 62.48.	
			M8 position 1500 rounds at B9a 65.42 – B9b 45.45 between 6 pm. + 12 midnight	
			M3 guns laid on S.O.S. line – did not fire	
			M1 GOZET M11 mounted for direct fire – did not fire	
			Intelligence NIL Casualties NIL	S.W.K.
In the LINE	13th		Weather Dull + wet Night firing carried out from M7 position M8 + M9:–	
			M7 500 rounds were fired at B9b 5.7. to B10.a. 2.5. between 9 pm + 3 am.	
			M8 1000 rounds fired at B10.a. 40.15. from 6 pm to 8 pm.	
			M9 1000 rounds fired on B9.a. 00.50 to B9.a. 62.48. between midnight + 4. am. 14th.	
			Intelligence NIL	
			Casualties NIL	S.W.K.

D. D. & L., London, E.C.
(A7883) Wt. W809/M1672 350,000 4/17 Sch. 52a Forms/C/2118/14

Instructions regarding War Diaries and Intelligence Summaries are contained in F. S. Regs., Part II. and the Staff Manual respectively. Title pages will be prepared in manuscript.

WAR DIARY
or
INTELLIGENCE SUMMARY.
(Erase heading not required.)

Army Form C. 2118.

Place	Date	Hour	Summary of Events and Information	Remarks and references to Appendices
In the LINE	14th		Weather :- Dull. No night firing	
			M1 GOZET M11 position. Guns laid for direct fire - did not fire	
			M3 M7 M8 M9 Guns laid on S.O.S. lines - did not fire	
			Intelligence NIL Casualties NIL	SAH
In the Line	15th		Weather :- Fine No night firing	
			M1 GOZET M11 position. Guns laid for direct fire - did not fire	
			M3 M7 M8 M9 Guns laid on S.O.S. lines - did not fire	
			Intelligence NIL Casualties NIL	SAH
In the Line	16th		Weather :- Fine Guns at M1 position moved to LE PONTCHU (B22 a 30 15 approx)	
			A A Gun at M8 position fired 100 rounds at E A but without effect	
			Between 5 p + 8 p.m. Enemy shelled B25 b + d + B26 a + c with 150 4.2 shell. During	
			the shelling a direct hit landed on roof of passage leading to O.C. Company's dugout. The passage	
			was roofed with elephant iron + earth. The whole lot caved in + filled up the passage	
			There were 20 casualties.	
			M1 GOZET M11 Guns mounted for direct fire - did not fire. M3 M7 M8 M9 laid on S.O.S. lines -	
			did not fire. Casualties NIL Intelligence NIL	SAH

D. D. & L., London, E.C.
(A7883) Wt. W809/M1672 350,000 4/17 Sch. 52a Forms/C/2118/14

Army Form C. 2118.

Instructions regarding War Diaries and Intelligence Summaries are contained in F. S. Regs., Part II, and the Staff Manual respectively. Title pages will be prepared in manuscript.

WAR DIARY
or
INTELLIGENCE SUMMARY.
(*Erase heading not required.*)

Place	Date	Hour	Summary of Events and Information	Remarks and references to Appendices
In the Line	17th		Weather Fine with Sunshine	
			A.A. gun in Reserve Line fired 250 rounds at E.A.	
			According to instruction from D.M.G.C. the 2 Guns in GOZET about B14 b 55.25 were withdrawn during the night + brought back to Coy Hdqrs.	
			M1 + M11 Guns laid for direct fire – did not fire	
			M3 M7 M8 M9 laid on S.O.S. lines – did not fire	
			Casualties NIL Intelligence NIL	[illegible]
In the Line	18th		Weather Fine with Sunshine	
			A.A. gun in RESERVE LINE fired 500 rounds at E.A. during the day	
			M1 + M11 positions. Guns laid for direct fire – did not fire	
			M3 M7 M8 M9 Guns laid on S.O.S. lines. Did not fire	
			Intelligence NIL Casualties NIL	[illegible]
In the Line	19th		Weather – Fine with Sunshine	
			M1 + M11 positions – Guns laid for direct fire – did not fire	
			M3 M7 M8 M9 – Guns laid on S.O.S. lines – did not fire	
			Intelligence NIL Casualties NIL	[illegible]

D. D. & L., London, E.C.
(A7883) Wt. W809/M1672 350,000 4/17 Sch. 52a Forms/C/2118/14

Instructions regarding War Diaries and Intelligence Summaries are contained in F. S. Regs., Part II. and the Staff Manual respectively. Title pages will be prepared in manuscript.

WAR DIARY
or
INTELLIGENCE SUMMARY.
(Erase heading not required.)

Army Form C. 2118.

Place	Date	Hour	Summary of Events and Information	Remarks and references to Appendices
In the Field	20th		Weather Fine with Sunshine.	
			M3 M7 M8 M9 positions Guns laid on S.O.S. lines — did not fire	
			M1 M11 positions Guns laid for direct fire — did not fire	
			Casualties NIL Intelligence NIL	SAH6
In the Field	21st		Weather :- Fine	
			A.A. Gun in reserve line fired 1000 rounds at E.A. during day but without result.	
			M1 + M11 Guns mounted for direct fire — did not fire	
			M3 M7 M8 M9 Guns laid for S.O.S. lines — did not fire	
			Intelligence NIL Casualties NIL	SAH6
In the Field	22nd		Weather :- Dull	
			M3 M7 M8 M9 Guns laid on S.O.S. lines — did not fire	
			M1 M11 Guns laid for direct fire — did not fire	
			Intelligence NIL Casualties NIL	SAH6
In the Field	23rd		Weather :- Dull	
			M3 M7 M8 M9 Guns laid on S.O.S. lines — did not fire	
			M1 M11 Guns laid for direct fire — did not fire	

D. D. & L., London, E.C.
(A7883) Wt. W809/M1672 350,000 4/17 Sch. 52a Forms/C/2118/14

Army Form C. 2118.

Instructions regarding War Diaries and Intelligence Summaries are contained in F. S. Regs., Part II. and the Staff Manual respectively. Title pages will be prepared in manuscript.

WAR DIARY
or
INTELLIGENCE SUMMARY.
(Erase heading not required.)

Place	Date	Hour	Summary of Events and Information	Remarks and references to Appendices
	23rd Contd.		Intelligence. – About a dozen H.E. Shells fell round the Entrance to Right Group Hdqrs. between 4 pm. + 4.30 pm.	
			Casualties NIL	[illegible]
In the Line	24th		Weather :- Fine with Sunshine	
			M1 + M11 Position. Guns laid for direct fire – did not fire.	
			~~X 2 pm~~ 8. pm 8 pm M11 guns relieved by 107th M. G. Coy. + proceeded with teams to Coy. Hdqrs.	
			M3 M7 M8 M9 Guns laid on S.O.S. line – did not fire.	
			Guns at M7 position relieved by 107th M.G. Coy at 8 pm. These guns then proceeded to their allotted positions in the Battle Zone A 29 d 3.2 + G 6 a 35.65 approximately.	
			The relief was carried out without incident	
			Intelligence NIL Casualties NIL	[illegible]
In the Line	25th		Weather :- Dull + Showery	
			M1 + Guns in Battle Zone laid for direct fire – did not fire	
			M3 M8 M9 Guns laid on S.O.S. line – did not fire	
			Intelligence: Nil Casualties NIL	[illegible]

D. D. & L., London, E.C.
(A7883) Wt. W809/M1672 350,000 4/17 Sch. 52a Forms/C/2118/14

Instructions regarding War Diaries and Intelligence Summaries are contained in F. S. Regs., Part II. and the Staff Manual respectively. Title pages will be prepared in manuscript.

WAR DIARY
or
INTELLIGENCE SUMMARY.
(*Erase heading not required.*)

Army Form C. 2118.

Place	Date	Hour	Summary of Events and Information	Remarks and references to Appendices
In the Line	26th ~~27th~~	Sat.	Weather:- Fine day with sunshine.	
			M1 & Guns in Battle Zone laid for direct fire. M3, M8 & M9 on S.O.S	
			line. Did not fire. Casualties - nil.	PA
	27th		Rainy morning with slight snow, afternoon fine, night frosty	
			Guns laid for direct & on S.O.S. line but did not fire	PA
	28th		Weather dull with some rain, night frosty.	
			Guns laid for direct fire & on S.O.S. barrage line. Did not fire.	
			S.O.S lines for M8 gun changed to B17a 68.92 — B17a 85.52.	
			Guns in Battle Zone were standing by ready to man position if	PA
			necessary	
			Company Strength :- 9 officers + 176 other ranks	
			Arthur Painting Lieut	
			Cmdg. 108th M. G. Coy	

D. D. & L., London, E.C.
(A7883) Wt. W809/M1672 350,000 4/17 Sch. 52a Forms/C/2118/14

C Coy 36 M. G. Battn

~~109th Machine Gun Company.~~

W A R D I A R Y

for

MONTH OF FEBRUARY, 1918.

Instructions regarding War Diaries and Intelligence Summaries are contained in F. S. Regs., Part II. and the Staff Manual respectively. Title pages will be prepared in manuscript.

WAR DIARY
or
~~INTELLIGENCE SUMMARY.~~
(Erase heading not required.)

Army Form C. 2118.

SHEET, I.

Place	Date	Hour	Summary of Events and Information	Remarks and references to Appendices
	FEBRUARY.			
HAPPENCOURT.	1st		Today, the Company carried on with Mechanism and SBR drill and inspection. The men inoculated yesterday are not very fit. Football in the afternoon. Very cold.	
	2nd		Work was carried out according to the training programme. The armourer sergeant is overhauling all tripods.	
	3rd		Church Parades for all denominations. A working party of about 40 ranks goes to work today on MG dugouts near URVILLERS. This greatly interferes with training.	
	4th		Parades according to programme. We find two AA guns here. Last night, HAM was bombed. The hostile planes pass over the village but it is very small.	
	5th		Work as per programme of training – this included Barrage Drill. We still provide the working party. The men are away for 12 hours. It is a long march. Capt MULHOLLAND returned from the Course at CAMIERS and resumed command of the Company.	
	6th		Company paraded under the CSM for an hour, chiefly for rifle drill as the guard carries rifles now and as some of the revolvers are to be withdrawn. Football.	
	7th		The C.O. took the Company at Barrage Drill with all the latest tips from CAMIERS. The Barrage Drill is splendid, including gun drill, use of angles and combines much useful gun work with smartness and all ranks have to think. All the stores left in BERTINCOURT dump arrived today.	

2353 Wt. W2544/1454 700,000 5/15 D. D. & L. A.D.S.S./Forms/C. 2118.

Instructions regarding War Diaries and Intelligence Summaries are contained in F. S. Regs., Part II. and the Staff Manual respectively. Title pages will be prepared in manuscript.

WAR DIARY
or
~~INTELLIGENCE~~ SUMMARY.

(*Erase heading not required.*)

Army Form C. 2118.

SHEET II.

Place	Date	Hour	Summary of Events and Information	Remarks and references to Appendices
	FEBRUARY.			
HAPPENCOURT.	8th		Work in camp according to programme. During the morning, the Officers & NCOs inspected the positions of the 107th MGCoy, as we take over in a few days.	
	9th		The men for inoculation had their second injection today. In the morning, work by programme. In the afternoon, the Battle Zone was reconnoitered – this in case of a serious hostile attack.	
	10th		Church Parades for all religions. The weather is damp and the village lies very low.	
	11th		All the men bathed today at ARTEMPS and blankets were steamed. After baths, the Company paraded under CSM. Reconnaissance of Battle Zone by Officers & NCOs at 2.0 p.m.	
	12th		At 10.0 a.m. the entire Company was inspected by Lt COL. de HOUGHTON, M.C., the DMGC.	
	13th		Today was very wet. Spare parts were very thoroughly overhauled & deficiencies made up as far as possible. We go in the line on the night 16th/17th Feb.	
	14th		The whole company carried out barrage drill in the morning. In the afternoon there was an intersection cross country run. A section winning with 61 points D section being second with 64 points.	
	15th		All available officers attended a lecture by the Divisional General at GRAND SERAUCOURT. The men carried out squad	[illegible]

2353 Wt. W2544/1454 700,000 5/15 D. D. & L. A.D.S.S./Forms/C. 2118.

Army Form C. 2118.

Instructions regarding War Diaries and Intelligence Summaries are contained in F. S. Regs., Part II. and the Staff Manual respectively. Title pages will be prepared in manuscript.

WAR DIARY
or
~~INTELLIGENCE SUMMARY.~~
(Erase heading not required.)

Place	Date	Hour	Summary of Events and Information	Remarks and references to Appendices
HAPPENCOURT	FEBRUARY 15th		drill and gun drill. In the afternoon the C.O. delivered a lecture to all officers & N.C.O's.	
IN THE LINE	16th		We relieved the 104th Company in the LEFT SUB SECTOR of the DIVISIONAL FRONT. A section took over positions 11 & 12, B & C sections took over positions 15, 16, 17 & 18 & D section positions 8 & 10. Relief was reported complete at 8.30 pm. At 11 pm the C.O. visited H.Q. of 15.16.17 & 18. A sections group of guns were agreed to call CENTRE GROUP, B & C sections LEFT GROUP & D sections guns RIGHT GROUP. RIGHT GROUP fired 2000 rounds on selected targets. At 11.15 pm RIGHT GROUP Headquarters were burnt down.	
	17th		A very cold morning 4° of frost being recorded. The C.O. visited CENTRE GROUP at 10.30 am. He also visited LEFT GROUP at 2.30 pm and Batt HQ at 5.30 pm.	
	18th		Still very cold. RIGHT GROUP visited by the C.O. Tests of S.O.S. signals were carried out at 10 pm. RIGHT GROUP	WB

2353 Wt. W2544/1454 700,000 5/15 D. D. & L. A.D.S.S./Forms/C. 2118.

Army Form C. 2118.

Instructions regarding War Diaries and Intelligence Summaries are contained in F. S. Regs., Part II. and the Staff Manual respectively. Title pages will be prepared in manuscript.

WAR DIARY
or
~~INTELLIGENCE SUMMARY.~~
(Erase heading not required.)

Place	Date	Hour	Summary of Events and Information	Remarks and references to Appendices
IN THE LINE	FEBRUARY		fired 2000 rounds on different targets.	
	19th		D.M.G.C. 36th Division D.M.G.C. 30th Division & Capt MULHOLLAND visited LEFT SECTOR which is going to be handed over to 30th Division.	
	20th		Nothing unusual occurred. Our guns fired a few thousand rounds on selected targets. We looked for a new Company H.Qtrs	
	21st		OC 89th Coy who are to relieve us on 23/24th, visited the LEFT SECTOR with Capt MULHOLLAND. LT WALKER reported from the CORPS CONFERENCE at Ham.	
	22nd		Two officers & a few men of the 89th Coy were accomodated in the LEFT SECTOR to received instruction in our dispositions N of the SOMME River. Our guns fired 3000 rounds on the usual targets.	
	23rd		The 89th Coy relieved our LEFT SECTOR. Relief reported complete at 9.30 pm. 2 Lt Sloan relieved Z section of the 266th Coy Relief complete at 11 pm. B section proceeded	W.B.

Instructions regarding War Diaries and Intelligence Summaries are contained in F. S. Regs., Part II. and the Staff Manual respectively. Title pages will be prepared in manuscript.

WAR DIARY
or
~~INTELLIGENCE SUMMARY.~~
(Erase heading not required.)

Army Form C. 2118.

Place	Date	Hour	Summary of Events and Information	Remarks and references to Appendices
IN THE LINE	FEBRUARY			
			to the Transport Lines	
	24th		"B" section proceeded to the BATTLE ZONE to occupy new positions. They were reported in position at 5.30 pm. To day proved rather uneventful	
	25th		LT ROBT reported from leave. LT WALKER proceeded on leave. 2 LT FOX came out of the line with a portion of D section for a rest. The 107th Coy took over our number 8 positions.	
	26th		Nothing of great importance occurred	
	27th		Infantry of 107th Bde caused a bit of excitement by "standing to" we drew loads of iron rations S.A.A. etc. The line again proved quiet	
	28th		CAPT MULHOLLAND is ordered to report to 35th M.G. Batt. LT BOWERBANK assumes command of the Coy. LT MILLS is second in command.	
			W Bowerbank Lt. 107th Machine Gun Coy.	

T2134. Wt. W708—776. 500000. 4/15. Sir J. C. & S.

Army Form C. 2118.

WAR DIARY
or
INTELLIGENCE SUMMARY.
(Erase heading not required.)

Instructions regarding War Diaries and Intelligence Summaries are contained in F. S. Regs., Part II. and the Staff Manual respectively. Title pages will be prepared in manuscript.

266 M G Coy — D Company 21st Battn M G Corps

Place	Date	Hour	Summary of Events and Information	Remarks and references to Appendices
Happencourt	12/2/18	[illegible]	In billets at Happencourt. Reserve gun positions occupied by half of Company	
Happencourt	13/2/18	[illegible]	— do — — do —	
Happencourt	14/2/18	[illegible]	— do — — do —	
Happencourt	15/2/18	[illegible]	— do — — do —	
Happencourt	16/2/18	[illegible]	One Section occupied positions at Grugies	
Happencourt	17/2/18	[illegible]	In billets & huts at Happencourt — do —	
Happencourt	18/2/18	[illegible]	— do —	
Happencourt	19/2/18	[illegible]	— do —	
Happencourt	20/2/18	[illegible]	— do —	
Happencourt	21/2/18	[illegible]	— do —	
Happencourt	22/2/18	[illegible]	— do —	
Happencourt	23/2/18	[illegible]	— do — All gun positions relieved by 109 M G Coy	
Happencourt	24/2/18	[illegible]	— do —	

A7092). Wt. W12839/M1293 750,000. 1/17. D. D & I. Ltd. Forms/C2118/14.

Instructions regarding War Diaries and Intelligence Summaries are contained in F. S. Regs., Part II. and the Staff Manual respectively. Title pages will be prepared in manuscript.

266 M G Coy

WAR DIARY
or
INTELLIGENCE SUMMARY.
(Erase heading not required.)

Army Form C. 2118.

[illegible] Company [illegible] Batt. M G Corps

Place	Date	Hour	Summary of Events and Information	Remarks and references to Appendices
Grand Séraucourt	1/2/18	[illegible]	In billets at Grand Séraucourt. Reserve gun positions occupied by [illegible] Company	
Grand Séraucourt	2/2/18	[illegible]	— do —	
Grand Séraucourt	3/2/18	[illegible]	— do —	
Grand Séraucourt	4/2/18	[illegible]	— do —	
Grand Séraucourt	5/2/18	[illegible]	— do —	
Grand Séraucourt	6/2/18	[illegible]	— do —	
Happencourt	7/2/18	9AM	Company moved into billets [illegible] at Happencourt — do —	
Happencourt	8/2/18	[illegible]	In billets at Happencourt — do —	
Happencourt	9/2/18	[illegible]	— do — — do —	
Happencourt	10/2/18	[illegible]	— do — — do —	
Happencourt	11/2/18	[illegible]	— do — — do —	

A7092. Wt. W12839/M1293 750,000. 1/17. D. D & L. Ltd. Forms/C2118/14.

Instructions regarding War Diaries and Intelligence Summaries are contained in F. S. Regs., Part II. and the Staff Manual respectively. Title pages will be prepared in manuscript.

WAR DIARY

or

INTELLIGENCE SUMMARY.

(Erase heading not required.)

Army Form C. 2118.

Place	Date	Hour	Summary of Events and Information	Remarks and references to Appendices
Happencourt	25/2/18	a/h	All Company in billets + huts at Happencourt	
Happencourt	26/2/18	a/h	— do —	
Happencourt	27/2/18	a/h	— do —	
Happencourt	28/2/18	a/h	— do —	

A7092. Wt. W12839/M1293 750,000. 1/17. D. D & L. Ltd. Forms/C2118/14.

Instructions regarding War Diaries and Intelligence Summaries are contained in F. S. Regs., Part II. and the Staff Manual respectively. Title pages will be prepared in manuscript.

266 MG Coy

WAR DIARY
or
INTELLIGENCE SUMMARY.

(Erase heading not required.)

266 M G Coy

Army Form C. 2118.

36

Place	Date	Hour	Summary of Events and Information	Remarks and references to Appendices
GRAND SÉRAUCOURT	1/2/18		In billets at GD. SÉRAUCOURT. Reserve gun positions occupied by half-company	
GRAND SÉRAUCOURT	2/2/18		— do —	
GRAND SÉRAUCOURT	3/2/18		— do —	
GRAND SÉRAUCOURT	4/2/18		— do —	
GRAND SÉRAUCOURT	5/2/18		— do —	
GRAND SÉRAUCOURT	6/2/18		— do —	
GRAND SÉRAUCOURT	7/2/18	9Am	Company moved into billets & huts at HAPPENCOURT — do —	
HAPPENCOURT	8/2/18		In billets at HAPPENCOURT — do —	
HAPPENCOURT	9/2/18		— do — — do —	
HAPPENCOURT	10/2/18		— do — — do —	
HAPPENCOURT	11/2/16		— do —	
HAPPENCOURT	12/2/18		— do — — do —	
HAPPENCOURT	13/2/18		— do — — do — — do —	

A7092. Wt. W12839/M1293 750,000. 1/17. D. D & I. Ltd. Forms/C2118/14.

Army Form C. 2[illegible]8.

Instructions regarding War Diaries and Intelligence Summaries are contained in F. S. Regs., Part II. and the Staff Manual respectively. Title pages will be prepared in manuscript.

266 MG Coy

WAR DIARY
or
INTELLIGENCE SUMMARY.
(Erase heading not required.)

Place	Date	Hour	Summary of Events and Information		Remarks and references to Appendices
HAPPENCOURT	14/2/18		In billets & huts at HAPPENCOURT	Reserve gun positions occupied by half coy.	
HAPPENCOURT	15/2/18		— do —	— do —	
HAPPENCOURT	16/2/18		— do —	One section occupied positions at GRUSIES ~~GRUSIES~~.	
HAPPENCOURT	17/2/18		In billets & huts at HAPPENCOURT	— do —	
HAPPENCOURT	18/2/18		— do —	— do —	
HAPPENCOURT	19/2/18		— do —	— do —	
HAPPENCOURT	20/2/18		— do —	— do —	
HAPPENCOURT	21/2/18		— do —	— do —	
HAPPENCOURT	22/2/18		— do —	— do —	
HAPPENCOURT	23/2/18		— do —	All gun positions relieved by 109 M. G. Coy.	
HAPPENCOURT	24/2/18		In billets & huts at HAPPENCOURT		
HAPPENCOURT	25/2/18		— do —		
HAPPENCOURT	26/2/18		— do —		
HAPPENCOURT	27/2/18		— do —		
HAPPENCOURT	28/2/18		— do —		
HAPPENCOURT	~~29/2/18~~ 1/3/18				

A7092. Wt. W12839/M1293 750,000. 1/17. D. D & L. Ltd. Forms/C2118/14.

SECRET

Reference Map
Gruges Ed. 2a.

Orders for Relief.

1. No. 107 M. G. Coy will be relieved in the line the night 16th/17th.

2. O.C. Right Group will detail two guides from each gun position to meet team from 109 M. G. Coy. at Crossroads A 17d. 90.40 at 6 pm.

3. O.C. No. 2 Section will detail one man from each gun team to meet incoming teams at Crossroads A 17d 90.40 at 6 pm.

4. O.C. Left Group will detail

one guide to be at HAM-ST. QUENTIN road by Coy. H.Q. at 6pm to guide 109 Coy. limber to Left Sector H.Q.

5. O.C. Left Sector will also detail one guide from each gun to be at Section H.Q. at 6pm. to conduct incoming teams to their respective positions.

6. O's.C. Right and Left Groups and O/c No. 2 Section will each detail one N.C.O., who is familiar with the positions, to remain until 9am. the 17th. when they will return to 109 Coy. H.Q., and return to 107 Coy. H.Q. at HAPPENCOURT

under the Senior N.C.O.

7. The following will be handed over on relief:
Range Cards, gun charts, programme of work in progress, and proposed, aiming posts, tripod T base, petrol tins, S.A.A., belts, gas alarms

8. Guns, tripods, belt boxes will be loaded on incoming Coy limbers.

9. On completion of relief Sections will return independently to Coy. H.Q. at HAPPENCOURT.

10. Completion of relief will be wired H.Q. using code word AMIENS

Acknowledge

Capt.
O.C. 10th Coy
M.G.C.

15/2/18

36th Divisional Troops.

Formed 1st March 1918 out of 107 108,109 & Machine Gun Companies.

))

36th BATTALION

MACHINE GUN ~~COMPANY~~ Corps

MARCH 1918

Appendices :-

Report on Operations 21st - 31st March.
Battalion Operation Order
Notes on Operations.
Trace - shewing gun positions.

"A" Coy 36th M.G. Battn

Vol I

WAR DIARY
or
INTELLIGENCE SUMMARY.
(Erase heading not required.)

Army Form C. 2118.

Instructions regarding War Diaries and Intelligence Summaries are contained in F. S. Regs., Part II. and the Staff Manual respectively. Title pages will be prepared in manuscript.

Place	Date	Hour	Summary of Events and Information	Remarks and references to Appendices
Field	1/3/18	[illegible]	Harassing fire in retaliation to enemy M.G. fire was started 15,150 rounds being fired. Day was quiet.	
	2/3/18	[illegible]	Day again quiet. No 6 position received a little attention from a 4.2 battery. 5,000 rounds fired during night. Enemy bombing planes again crossed our lines in the evening.	
	3/3/18	[illegible]	Period quiet. Enemy machine guns less active [illegible] harassing fire 5,000 rounds were fired. Aircraft active.	
	4/3/18	[illegible]	Day & night again quiet except for [illegible] gun fire which was replied to by our guns. 8,000 rounds [illegible] fired.	
	5/3/18	[illegible]	A few shells near [illegible] guns. Aircraft again active [illegible] crossed our lines low but was driven off under heavy [illegible] fire. [illegible] active [illegible] at night [illegible] 13,000 rounds during the evening.	
	6/3/18	[illegible]	[illegible] near No 6 gun. Enemy again active. Enemy machine guns less active. Our guns fired 7,500 rounds [illegible].	

D. D. & L., London, E.C.
(A7883) Wt W809/M1672 350,000 4/17 Sch. 52a Forms/C/2118/14

6

Instructions regarding War Diaries and Intelligence Summaries are contained in F. S. Regs., Part II. and the Staff Manual respectively. Title pages will be prepared in manuscript.

WAR DIARY
or
~~INTELLIGENCE SUMMARY.~~
(*Erase heading not required.*)

Vol 3 — Army Form C. 2118.

36th Bn M.G.C.

Place	Date	Hour	Summary of Events and Information	Remarks and references to Appendices
Field	1 March	1 pm	36th Bn. Machine Gun Corps formed with H.Q. at HAPPENCOURT	
			O.C. LT COL G. DE HOGHTON M.C. 2nd in Command.	
			MAJOR LOW M.C. Adjutant LT J WILSON	
			LT + QM. T BARRETT.	
			Company Commanders:- A Co. CAPT. T.E. FITZGERALD	
			B Co. " MOORHOUSE	
			C Co. " MULHOLLAND	
			D Co. MAJOR GAUNTLETT	
			The formation of the Battn coincides with the reorganisation of the Division + the extra personnel to complete establishments is drawn from the disbanded Batts.	
			A B + C Cos in the line having a total of 30 guns in the forward Zone + 20 guns in the battle Zone	
			D Co in Div. reserve at HAPPENCOURT.	

D. D. & L., London, E.C. (A7883) Wt W8c9/M1672 350,000 4/17 Sch. 52a Forms/C/2118/14

Army Form C. 2118.

Instructions regarding War Diaries and Intelligence Summaries are contained in F. S. Regs., Part II. and the Staff Manual respectively. Title pages will be prepared in manuscript.

WAR DIARY
or
INTELLIGENCE SUMMARY. 36th Bn M. G. C.

(Erase heading not required.)

Place	Date	Hour	Summary of Events and Information	Remarks and references to Appendices
Field	2nd	PM	Harassing fire carried out on trenches, tracks behind enemy lines – normal day.	
	3rd		Usual programme of harassing fire carried out.	
	4th	PM	D Co relieved B Co in right Bde sector of the line	
	5th	PM	Programme of harassing fire on tracks, roads etc behind enemy lines	
	6th	PM	Usual night firing programme carried out	
	7th	PM	Programme of harassing M.G. fire carried out on tracks, roads & HQ. Enemy aeroplanes exceedingly active 18 planes crossing our lines by day. One E.A. dropped bombs near GRUGIES.	
	8th	PM	11,400 rds fired on targets X roads etc behind enemy lines during the night. Bombing planes crossed our lines continuously up to midnight.	
	9th	PM	13,000 rounds fired on targets behind enemy lines. Aircraft on both sides very active by day.	

D. D. & L., London, E.C. (A7883) Wt W809/M1672 350,000 4/17 Sch. 52a Forms/C/2118/14

Instructions regarding War Diaries and Intelligence Summaries are contained in F. S. Regs., Part II, and the Staff Manual respectively. Title pages will be prepared in manuscript.

WAR DIARY
or
~~INTELLIGENCE SUMMARY.~~
(Erase heading not required.)

36th Bn M. G. C

Army Form C. 2118.

Place	Date	Hour	Summary of Events and Information	Remarks and references to Appendices
Field	10th	pm	14,000 rds fired on targets behind enemy lines	
			Small fires observed in ST QUENTIN at night	
	11th	pm	2,500 rds fired on centre of activity in enemy lines during the night.	
	12th	pm	4000 rds fired on roads & centres of activity behind enemy lines. An enemy plane brought down behind enemy lines by two of ours at 6.15 P.M. abt 57c. Fire observed in direction of ST QUENTIN	
	13th	pm	4000 rds fired on roads & tracks behind enemy lines	
			Enemy plane forced to land by 3 of ours about 6.50 P.M.	
			A small red balloon landed in our lines with 3 copies of Gazette des ARDENES attached	
	14th	pm	2,000 rds fired on X roads & trench in enemy line	
			A large fire was observed to break out in St QUENTIN	
	15th	pm	9000 rds on trenches & roads behind enemy lines	

D. D. & L., London, E.C.
(A7883) Wt W8co/M1672 250,000 4/17 Sch. 52a Forms/C/2118/14

Army Form C. 2118.

Instructions regarding War Diaries and Intelligence Summaries are contained in F. S. Regs., Part II. and the Staff Manual respectively. Title pages will be prepared in manuscript.

WAR DIARY

or

~~INTELLIGENCE SUMMARY.~~

(Erase heading not required.)

36th B.M.G.C.

Place	Date	Hour	Summary of Events and Information	Remarks and references to Appendices
Field	16th	PM	11,500 rds fired on targets behind enemy lines. Artillery much quieter on both sides	
	17th	PM	12,200 rds fired on usual Targets. Considerable activity seen behind enemy lines. Great aerial activity on both sides	
	18th	PM	10,500 rds fired on usual Targets. Aircraft normal. Enemy fired numerous flares during the night	
	19th	PM	6,500 rds fired on usual targets. Enemy aircraft inactive	
	20th	PM	Uneventful day, nothing unusual happened	

D. D. & L., London, E.C.
(A7883) Wt W8c9/M1672 350,000 4/17 Sch. 52a Forms/C/2118/14

Programme of Work

Week ending March, 1st, 1918.

Time	Monday	Tuesday	Wednesday	Thursday	Friday	Saturday
7.30 - 7.45 am	Running Exercise	Running Exercise	Running Exercise	Running Exercise	—	Running Exercise
7.30 - 8.0 am	Riding Parade (Officers)	—	Riding Parade (Officers)	—	—	Riding Parade (Officers)
9 a.m.	Inspection of Coy.	Inspection of Coy.	Inspection of Coy.	Inspection of Coy	Inspection of Coy	—
9.15 - 12.30	Classes for new attached men	Classes for new attached men		Classes for new men	Classes for new men	10.30 a.m. Kit Inspection
9 - 9.30	Squad Drill Drivers	Arms Drill - Drivers		Saluting Drill (drivers)	Saluting Drill (drivers)	11-1 Sections at disposal of Section Officers.
9.15 - 10.	Immediate Action	Mechanism	Route March	Stoppages	Stoppages F.A.	
10 - 10.45	Gun Drill	Gun drill with light mounting		Rough Ground Drill	Advanced Gun drill	
11 - 11.30	P.T.	P.T.		P.T.	P.T.	
11.40 - 12.30	Barrage drill	Barrage Drill		Barrage drill	Barrage Drill	Classes for new men
12.30 - 1 p.m.	Cleaning of guns & packing in limbers	Cleaning of guns & packing in limbers		Cleaning guns and packing in limbers	Cleaning guns & packing in limbers	
Afternoon	Section Football	Paper chase	Recreation	5.30 p.m. - Night operation*	Football	Section Football

* I propose to take Coy. to gun positions in the Battle Zone.

S E C R E T.   Copy No 11

No.36 Battalion Machine Gun Corps Order No 1.

Rof.Map 62.c.N.W.1/20,000

1. - On the night 4/5th March 1918, D Coy will relieve B Coy in the line and Battle Zone.

2. - Guides as under will be required and will be at the Cross Roads in B.26.b. at 7 p.m. on 4th March.

From No 1 position - 1 guide.
" " 2 " - 2 guides,
" " 3 " - 1 guide,
" "
From FOUCHARD Trench - 1 guide.

3. - All trench stores, including T bases, S.A.A. in bulk and Reserve water and rations will be handed over, a list of the above stores and receipts being forwarded to Hd.Qrs. by 6 p.m. 5th March.

4. - All belts, guns, tripods, etc. will be brought out of the line by B Coy.

5. - Trench Maps, Range Cards, etc. and all details as to S.O.S. lines to be handed over.

6. - One man from each incoming team will spend the day of the 4th March at each position to be taken over.

7. - All further details of relief to be arranged between Coys concerned.

8. - Battalion Transport Officer will ~~arrange~~ provide sufficient limbers to take in D Coy and bring back B Coys Stores.

9. - Completion of relief will be wired to Hd.Qrs. by code work 'INK'

10.- ACKNOWLEDGE.

-------------------2nd Lt & A/Adjt.

3rd March 1918.   for O.C. No 36 Batt. Machine Gun Corps.

Copy No 1 to Commanding Officer,
2 to Headquarters,
3 to A Coy,
4 to B "
5 to C "
6 to D "
7 to 36th Div.
8 to 36th Div. Signals,
9 to 108th Inf. Bde.
10 to Transport Officer,
11 to War Diary,
12 to File.

36 Battn. Machine Gun Corps.

WAR DIARY. Period 21st. - 31st. March.

21st.	When the German offensive commenced B. C. and D. Coys. were in the Line with A. Coy. in Divisional Reserve at HAPPENCOURT. D. Coy. was on the Right Bde. front, B. Coy. Centre Bde. front, and C. Coy. Left Bde. front.
5 a.m.	Enemy barrage opened and the first shell fell in HAPPENCOURT at the same time, killing 3 and wounding 10 men at Battn. Headquarters.
5-30 a.m.	"Man Battle Stations" received. A. Coy. moved to G.36. under Lieut. Bolton and the remaining Battn. Transport to TUGNY et PONT under Major Low. 2 Guns under Lieut. K. HANSELL moved to position at ESSIGNY STATION. Enemy still continued to shell HAPPENCOURT.
6-30 a.m.	Dull misty morning, impossible to see more than 100 yds. Battn. H.Q. moved to 109th. Inf. Bde. H.Q. in the Quarry at HAMEL LOCK.
7 a.m.	In touch with the four Company Commanders at their respective Bde. H.Q's. A. Coy. ordered to man the Redoubt Line, Battle Zone. 3 Drivers and 10 Mules wounded at G.3.b. while waiting for this order. Little information from Forward Zone due to intensity of enemy artillery fire. All forward buried cable broken. Nos. 3. and 8 Guns destroyed, the mist ~~preventing~~ hiding the approach of the enemy. No 9 Gun destroyed by shell fire and replaced by 1 gun and gun team from A. Coy.
10 a.m.	Guns No 9 and 11 destroyed by heavy shelling of their positions and No. 13 and 14 withdrawn to the quarry at B.27.b. to escape a similar fate.
11 p.m.	Infantry retired on the flanks and left No 11 and 12 guns exposed. Enemy bombed down trench and captured the guns. M.5. gun destroyed by shell fire about this time leaving a total of 7 guns in centre sector. These guns reinforced by one gun team which succeeded in returning from GRUGIES together with the surviving guns of A. and C. Coys retired and took up positions with the Infantry on the HAPPENCOURT - HAMEL road, west of the Canal. Battn. H.Q. evacuated the Quarry at HAMEL LOCK and proceeded to PITHON with the Transport and Battn. details.
22nd. 12-30 p.m.	Guns retired with the Infantry to new line 600 yds. in rear of HAPPENCOURT.
7-30 p.m.	Enemy attacked and three guns were destroyed. Battn. H.Q. moved via HAM to GOLANCOURT. The 23 remaining guns with the Battn. moved across the river with the Infantry and took up positions in BROUCHY, CUGNY, and in front of the railway embankment betweeb EAUCOURT and OLLEZY. Infantry line reorganised with 2 guns under Lieut. KITCHEN on the left flank in front of EAUCOURT and 2 guns under Lieut. BOLTON on railway embankment South of SOMMETTE EAUCOURT
10 p.m.	Infantry retired to Line at MONTALIMONT FARM and above mentioned guns moved to positions in the line.

23rd.	Transport moved to FRENISHES and later to FRETOY le CHATEAU. 121, 122, 150 Coys. R.E. with details from M.G.Battn. and Stragglers from various Units were collected under Major Low and held a line from a point 1000 yds. west of BROUCHY through the North end of GOLANCOURT to Fme de BONNEUIL thence to a point 500 yds. West of BONNEUIL CHATEAU. 121 Coy. R.E. was in touch with Div. details on the Left.
11 p.m.	Enemy attacked this line between GOLANCOURT and BROUCHY forcing it to retire on to the prepared FRENCH line behind.
24th.	Guns under Lieuts. BOLTON and KITCHEN retired with the Infantry to a line in front of VILLESELVE.
3 p.m.	Lieut. BOLTON wounded and 2 guns destroyed.
4 p.m.	2 guns under Lieut. KITCHEN retired to a ridge West of VILLESELVE.
5 p.m.	General retirement through BERLANCOURT and GUISCARD.
25th.	Battn. H.Q. and Transport moved to MARGNY where Coys. rejoined and were organised into 3 Coys. each of 4 guns.
6 p.m.	Battn. moved to GUERBIGNY arriving about 2 a.m. 26th.
26th.	Orders received to take up a line BOUCHOIR ERCHES to a point R.19.a. (Sheet 66.E. Ed.1.) A. Coy. of 4 guns was attached to each Inf. Bde. Battn. H.Q. remained with 107th. Inf. Bde. H.Q. at Cross Roads Q.22.b. (Sheet 66.E.) but moved later in the day to Quarry at Q.2.a. The Battn. details under Lieuts. WALKER and KITCHEN were attached to 1st. R.I.Rifles. Enemy brought up heavy T.Ms. into ERCHES during the night and caused casualties. Enemy patrol attacked 108th. Inf. Bde. H.Q. where O.C. B. Coy. Capt. MOOREHOUSE had his H.Q.
27th.	Enemy launched attack. Guns retired with the Infantry and fell back in the evening on a line previously prepared by the 30th. Division in front of HANGEST. The Coy. under Lieut. MUNN attached to 109th. Inf. Bde. covered the retirement of that Bde. across the river. Guns were mounted on Limbers and galloped back to take up new positions. At the fourth stage of the retirement the guns passed through a FRENCH Section already in position. All Coys. when relieved by the FRENCH marched to SOURDON.
29th.	Orders were received at 12 noon to take up a position in front of COULLEMELLE to cover deployments of R.F.A. and FRENCH Artillery. 7 guns marched out under Lieut. Colonel de HOGHTON, divided into 3 sections under Captain MOOREHOUSE with Lieuts. WALKER, HOWIE and FOX. 2 guns were posted on each flank of the line with the remaining three in the centre. The guns remained in position all night and at 8 a.m. 2 guns under Lieut. WALKER and 2 guns under 2nd. Lt. FOX were ordered to take up positions on two small copses on either side of the road to VILLERS - TURNEL about 1 Km. short of the village. In each case the guns had an escort of Infantry. All 7 guns were withdrawn about noon and marched to EPAGNY where the Transport was already quartered.
9 p.m.	Battn. moved to WAILLY arriving about 5 a.m. 30th.
30th.	Battn. moved to SALEUX to entrain for GAMACHE
31st.	Battn. entrained at 11-30 a.m. and arrived at EU about 6 p.m. marched to Billets in BOURSEVILLE.

No. 36 Battn. Machine Gun Corps.

NARRATIVE OF EVENTS 21 - 31 MARCH.

From 4.30 a.m. on the morning of 21st March only one Runner succeeded in reaching his Coy. H.Q. He came to H.Q. 108th Inf. Brigade where O.C. "D" Coy. 36th Battn. Machine Gun Corps had his H.Q.

The report he brought stated that certain areas were being heavily shelled with H.E. and Gas Shells. The gun teams in the vicinity of JEAN D'ARC reported heavy shelling with gas, and ESSIGNY STATION guns reported heavy shelling with H.E. No casualties were reported up to that time.

No message was received subsequent to that, but from statements by survivors the enemy seems to have bombed down the C.Ts. in the Forward Zone.

ESSIGNY STATION.

About 8.30 a.m. two guns of "A" Coy. E. of the railway cutting at ESSIGNY STATION saw the Infantry of the 14th Division retiring and they stated that the enemy had taken ESSIGNY VILLAGE. About 9 a.m. enemy advanced from the Village in the direction of the Station and at the same time information was received that he was making his way down the Railway Cutting. One gun was mounted on the side of the Railway Cutting to stop this latter movement, and half an hour later a large body of the enemy approached. When it became certain that they were Germans, fire was opened on them and they dispersed.

Several of the enemy entered a trench on the W. side of the Railway and fired on the gun, killing the No. 1 and 2 of the team.

The remaining gun worked by Lieut. K.J.N. HANSELL stopped the movement of the enemy towards ESSIGNY STATION and did great execution for ¾ of an hour when Lieut. HANSELL was killed and the gun destroyed.

The gun was withdrawn from the cutting about 11.30 a.m. and took up a new position 50 yds. away on the W. side of it, and continued to engage the enemy advancing from ESSIGNY VILLAGE, causing him heavy losses.

About 3 p.m. the Sergt. in Command asked a unit of the 14th Division to send a Lewis Gun forward to hold the railway cutting and a few Infantry men to protect him from snipers. The O.C. complied with this request but in the meantime a German Machine Gun had commenced to fire down the cutting and prevented the Lewis Gun from coming into action.

About 6 p.m. our Artillery opened on ESSIGNY STATION and an Enemy shell which fell short completely destroyed the enemy gun. The Lewis Gun was then mounted to sweep the cutting.

Our gun withdrew about 11 p.m. in the general retirement.

BATTLE ZONE.

About 10.45 a.m. the enemy was first seen by the guns in the Battle Zone. The heavy mist allowed the enemy to approach to within 200 yds. of the guns unobserved.

The guns on the right opened fire on parties of the enemy in considerable strength advancing from the direction of the railway cutting, and inflicted heavy casualties.

Sniping commenced at once and 2 gunners under 2nd Lieut. J.R. SMITH were killed.

The enemy succeeded on the Right of the Division Front in almost every case in penetrating into the trenches, and bombed his way down. In this way No. 5 gun was cut off, being situated in the vertical shaft of a Champagne Dugout, out in front of the trench. The gun team destroyed the gun and succeeded in rejoining another Section.

The enemy penetrated into the Chamber of the Champagne Dugout occupied by 2nd Lieut. SMITH and sniped both gunners at the top of the vertical shaft. This gun was successfully withdrawn to another position.

The surviving guns covered the retirement of the Infantry across the River, and took up positions in the new line.

The guns were rearranged by Lieut.Colonel de. HOGHTON on the morning of the 22nd.

The guns covered the retirement of the Infantry to a new line behind HAPPENCOURT and prevented several attempts by the enemy to follow up. One gun fired with effect on parties of the enemy crossing a foot bridge near ARTEMPS.

Enemy aircraft was exceedingly active during the day, flying low and firing into the Trenches.

Enemy Infantry advanced about 6 p.m. and made good Machine Gun targets, This attempt was repeated but broke down under Machine Gun fire each time.

Several Enemy Infantry succeeded in entering our trenches eventually and proceeded to bomb as usual.

The Infantry retired and two gunners were killed before they could remove their guns.

2 guns with the 2nd Royal Irish Rifles were in action all day and held up an enemy flanking movement for several hours.

Two guns lost touch, and joined up with the 30th Division and fought through AUBIGNY with them. The Officer in Command states that the enemy used Motor Machine Guns at that place.

<u>23rd.</u> The Infantry fell back steadily and crossed the River, the Machine Guns covering the retirement. One gun was destroyed during this operation.

The guns took up position in the new line, 2 on the CUGNY Main Road N. of EAUCOURT, and 4 around the Village with the 9th Royal Irish Fus. and 2 on the left flank of the 9th R. Inniskilling Fusiliers.

Our left flank retired from AUBIGNY but a counter attack retook the Village. One Machine Gun under 2nd Lieut. EVANS assisted in this attack.

<u>24th.</u> The whole line withdrew to VILLESELVE and took up positions on the ridge W. of the Village where the Machine Guns joined after covering the retirement. One gun was put out of action during this movement.

One gun under Lieut. KITCHEN did some execution at this place. Parties of the enemy continually attempted to cross a road and each time were mown down by his fire.

An enemy Machine Gun was brought into position and fired several belts, searching for our gun. Lieut. KITCHEN spotted the position by the escape of steam from the barrel casing, and engaged it. The gun did not fire again.

The experiences of all gun teams during this part of the operations were very similar. No large targets of the enemy presented themselves.

On the morning of the 23rd three Field Coys.,121st, 122nd and 150th, with the details of the Machine Gun Battalion took up a line from a point 1,000 yds. West of BROUCHY through the North end of GOLANCOURT to Fme de BOURSEVILLE thence to a point 500 yds. West of BOURSEVILLE Chateau. At this point the left of the 121st Coy. R.E. was in touch with the Division Details Battalion.

The enemy attacked this line between GOLANCOURT and BROUCHY and penetrated and proceeded to work round the right flank. The line retired on to the prepared French Line behind and remained there until 8 p.m. the next evening when the whole line retired again.

That night the remaining teams were withdrawn from the line and marched to SERMAIZE.

<u>25th.</u> The Battalion reorganised next day at MARGNY into 3 Coys. each of 4 guns and marched to GUERBIGNY that night.

At 9 a.m. next morning orders were received to take up positions in the line BOUCHOIR - ERCHES to a point R.19.a. 'A' Coy. of 4 guns was attached to each Infantry Brigade. The details of the Battalion were attached to the 1st Royal Irish Rifles as Infantry.

The day was uneventful but at dusk 2 gun teams with the R.E. Field Coys. and the Pioneer Battalion in front of ERCHES saw a Cavalry Patrol said to be French operating to their front. Shortly afterwards a party of Infantry in fours advanced down a road towards our lines with protecting flanking parties out. This party was also said to be French but one of our Infantry fired on them and the advancing party fired from the hip in return, while still on the move.

The R.E. Officer in Command of the Section ordered the Infantry to retire on the right and they withdrew to a Line behind ERCHES.

A German Cavalry Patrol approached from the rear and endeavoured to pass through to their own lines. They were challenged but did not reply and were fired on. One trooper was killed, the remainder escaped.

At night the enemy brought up T.Ms. and Field Guns into the Village and attacked about 8.30 next morning. The Infantry again retired covered by Machine Gun fire.

About 11 a.m. a party of the enemy succeeded in working round behind our lines and endeavoured to attract attention, waving with flags and shouting. At the same time an attack was launched from the front. The party under Lieuts. WALKER and KITCHEN left their trenches and charged. The enemy fell back into ERCHES pursued by this party. On entering the Village our men came under heavy M.G. fire and were forced to retire.

The whole line retired later in the day to a line South of ARVILLERS and fell back in the evening to a line in front of HANGEST prepared by the 30th Division.

The Coy. attached to the 109th Inf. Brigade covered the retirement of that Brigade across the river. Guns were mounted on limbers and galloped back to new positions in rear. At the fourth stage of the retirement this Coy. passed through a French Maitrailleuse Section already in position.

29th. The Coys. rejoined the Battalion at SOURDON. At 12 noon 7 guns marched out to take up a position in front of CAULLEMELLE to cover the deployment of R.F.A. and French Artillery. They remained in position till noon 30th when they withdrew and marched to EPAGNY.

This finished the active operations of the Battalion.

NOTES ON RECENT FIGHTING AS REGARDS MACHINE GUNS. LESSONS LEARNT AND SUGGESTIONS.

1. System of Machine Gun defence in depth must break down in either dark, or fog. Nearly all guns of this battalion placed in Forward Zone were captured probably without firing a shot, owing to not being able to see. Those laid on S.O.S. lines presumably fired for only a short time and then prepared for direct targets.

2. Where guns are placed to defend "redoubts" etc. they must be in view of other guns on either flank to give each other mutual support as they cannot fire in all directions at once and so defend themselves.

3. Communication must be by runner, runners themselves being highly trained and reliable men and not those selected because they are not considered good gunners. On the whole communication was not good chiefly owing no doubt to the fact that no Headquarters were ever permanent.

4. Necessity of large supply of loaded reserve belts, as in a retirement all or nearly all empty belts and boxes are left behind, teams becoming small there are not sufficient men to carry everything back.

5. In many cases the Machine Guns were the last to leave covering by their fire (direct) the withdrawal of the Infantry.

6. All Machine Gun ammunition should be in belts. If this had been the case several more guns could have, at various times, been utilized. There were no reserve belts in the Army Park.

7. A mobile reserve should be kept if in any waypossible by O.C. Battalion. If I had had 8 guns under my hand there were innumerable opportunities of inflicting heavy losses on the enemy - especially as at times we had no supporting Artillery.

(Sgd) G. de HOGHTON,
Lt. Col.,
36th M. G. Battn.

66^C N.W.
66^D N.E. } PARTS of

REFERENCE

ALTERNATIVE POSITIONS

Officers DUGOUT

SCALE 1/20,000

All positions single guns
Except where otherwise stated.

36th Divisional Machine Guns.

36th BATTALION MACHINE GUN CORPS

APRIL 1918.

No 36 Bn Machine Gun Corps. **WAR DIARY** or **INTELLIGENCE SUMMARY.** April 1918. Army Form C. 2118.

Instructions regarding War Diaries and Intelligence Summaries are contained in F. S. Regs., Part II. and the Staff Manual respectively. Title pages will be prepared in manuscript.

(Erase heading not required.)

Vol 3

Place	Date	Hour	Summary of Events and Information	Remarks and references to Appendices
In the Field.	1/4/18.	[illegible]	Battalion billeted in BOURSEVILLE.	
			Re-distribution of Mobilization stores by Bn Quartermaster.	
			Lieut R.B.S. MUNN appointed to command C Coy vice Lt C. SAXBY wounded. Lieut H.M. KITCHEN appointed 2nd in Command B Coy. vice Lt TAINTING wounded. Lieut F. MILLS appointed 2nd in C. A Coy vice Lt BOLTON wounded	
	2/4/18.	[illegible]	Re-distribution of mobilization stores continued. A number of N.C.O's & men of A B & C Coys transferred to D Coy. to equalise Coys. Warning order received from Division to be prepared to move North.	
	3/4/18.	[illegible]	Orders for entraining received. A Coy entrained at FEUQUIERES at 6 pm. B Coy at WOINCOURT at 7 pm, C Coy at EU at 8 pm.	
	4/4/18.	[illegible]	Entraining continued. D Coy entrained at WOINCOURT at 7am. Bn Hd Qrs at FEUQUIERES at 9am. – Detraining – A Coy detrained at PROVEN at 7am. B Coy at ROUSBRUGGE at	

(A9175) Wt W2358/P360 600,000 12/17 D. D. & L. Sch. 52a. Forms/C2118/15

Instructions regarding War Diaries and Intelligence Summaries are contained in F. S. Regs., Part II, and the Staff Manual respectively. Title pages will be prepared in manuscript.

WAR DIARY

or

~~INTELLIGENCE SUMMARY.~~

(Erase heading not required.)

Army Form C. 2118.

Place	Date	Hour	Summary of Events and Information	Remarks and references to Appendices
	4/4/18.	F.W.J.	9am. C Coy at REXPOEDE at 11am. These Coys were taken by lorries from their respective stations to BRAKE CAMP. Orders received from Division that 31 guns would relieve a similar number of guns of the 1st Battalion on the night 6/7th April.	
	5/4/18	F.W.J.	Bn Hd Qrs detrained at PROVEN at 7am. D Coy at ROUSBRUGGE at 8am and proceeded by lorries to BRAKE CAMP. 1 officer and 8 gunners from A B & C Coys proceeded to the line to reconnoitre gun positions and remain in the line.	
	6/4/18.	F.W.J.	15 officers and 269 OR. reinforcements joined from Base Depot. Bn moved from BRAKE CAMP, A & B Coys going into the line, and C & D Coys with Bn Hd Qrs proceeded to TURCO HUTS. C Coy to man Battle Zone if required. Transport lines at BRIELIN Cross Roads.	
	7/4/18.	F.W.J.	A & B Coys in the line. Nothing unusual occurred. Our artillery fired all day on the enemy's back area.	

(A9175) Wt W2358/P563 600,000 12/17 D. D. & L. Sch 52a. Forms/C2118/15

Instructions regarding War Diaries and Intelligence Summaries are contained in F. S. Regs., Part II, and the Staff Manual respectively. Title pages will be prepared in manuscript.

WAR DIARY

~~or~~

~~INTELLIGENCE SUMMARY.~~

(*Erase heading not required.*)

Army Form C. 2118.

Place	Date	Hour	Summary of Events and Information	Remarks and references to Appendices
	8/4/18.	F.W.J.	Very quiet on both sides. 11 N.C.O. reinforcements arrived from Base and were posted to Coys as follows:- 2 cpls & 1 L/cpl to "A" Coy, 3 L/cpls to "B" Coy, 1 cpl & 1 L/cpl to "C" Coy. 1 Sgt & 2 cpls to "D" Coy.	
	9/4/18.	F.W.J.	Both sides very active with artillery & machine guns. Lieut. J. WILSON appointed A/Capt. whilst employed as Adjutant of the Bn. d. 24/3/18.	
	10/4/18.	F.W.J.	At 11 am. orders were received from the Division that 1 Coy would "Stand To" ready to move off at a moment's notice. "C" Coy warned to "Stand To". At 1.50 pm. wire received from Div. ordering "C" Coy to proceed by lorry to KEMMEL and to be at the disposal of IX th Corps. "C" Coy moved off at 2.30 pm.	
	11/4/18.	F.W.J.	Our guns fired 1000 rds on TAPA FARM to which the enemy quickly retaliated. Lt. MUNN & 2/Lt. FOX with 4 new guns joined "C" Coy at KEMMEL. 12 new guns complete issued to "D" Coy and 1 to "B" Coy. Bn now complete with guns, etc.	

(A9475) Wt W2358/P360 600,000 12/17 D. D. & L. Sch. 52a. Forms/C2118/15

Instructions regarding War Diaries and Intelligence Summaries are contained in F. S. Regs., Part II. and the Staff Manual respectively. Title pages will be prepared in manuscript.

WAR DIARY or ~~INTELLIGENCE~~ SUMMARY.

(Erase heading not required.)

Army Form C. 2118.

Place	Date	Hour	Summary of Events and Information	Remarks and references to Appendices
	12/4/18.	F.W.J.	Very quiet day. 2/Lt A.T. HUGHES reported from Base Depot & posted to D Coy.	
	13/4/18.	F.W.J.	D Coy occupied the positions in the Battle Zone during the day. During the night 13/14th B Coy relieved 8 guns of A Coy., the remaining guns of A & B Coys remained as before. The following Officers reported from the Base and were posted to Coys as follows:- Lieut W.J. HOPPER to B Coy, 2/Lt R.B. HAMILTON to C Coy, 2/Lt H. HEMINGWAY to D Coy.	
	14/4/18	F.W.J.	Very quiet day. Bn Hd Qrs moved from TURCO HUTS to CANAL BANK.	
	15/4/18.	F.W.J.	During the afternoon D Coy took over 6 guns positions from 41st Bn M.G.C. During the night 15/16th the 16 guns East of STEENBEEK were withdrawn to CANAL BANK according to Order No 8.	
	16/4/18.	F.W.J.	Enemy artillery very active during the day & night. No casualties	
	17/4/18	F.W.J.	Enemy again very active with artillery fire. 6 guns of D Coy relieved by 18th Regt, 4th Belgian Division during night in	

(A9475) Wt W2358/P360 600,000 12/17 D. D. & L. Sch. 52a. Forms/C2118/15

Instructions regarding War Diaries and Intelligence Summaries are contained in F. S. Regs., Part II, and the Staff Manual respectively. Title pages will be prepared in manuscript.

WAR DIARY
or
~~INTELLIGENCE SUMMARY.~~

(*Erase heading not required.*)

Army Form C. 2118.

Place	Date	Hour	Summary of Events and Information	Remarks and references to Appendices
	17/4/18.	F.W.J.	accordance with Order No 9.	
	18/4/18	F.W.J.	Our artillery was very active all day. The Bosche was also very active, paying special attention to BOUNDRY Road, BUFF's Road and HILL TOP.	
	19/4/18.	F.W.J.	Both sides very active with artillery and machine guns.	
	20/4/18.	F.W.J.	Enemy aircraft rather more active than usual. Our A.A. guns had some good targets and with tracer ammunition some good shooting was observed.	
	21/4/18.	F.W.J.	Our guns at CHEDDAR VILLA fired 3,000 rds on enemy's position during the night to which the enemy retaliated with his M.G's and artillery.	
	22/4/18	F.W.J.	'B' Coy relieved 'A' Coy in the Reserve line as detailed in Order No 10.	
	23/4/18	F.W.J.	Re-organisation of guns took place on the night 22/23rd, during the 23rd and the night 23/24th. Details of the re-organisation are given in Order No 11.	

(A9475) Wt W2358/P360 600,000 12/17 D. D. & L. Sch 52a. Forms/C2118/15

Instructions regarding War Diaries and Intelligence Summaries are contained in F. S. Regs., Part II. and the Staff Manual respectively. Title pages will be prepared in manuscript.

WAR DIARY
or
~~INTELLIGENCE SUMMARY.~~
(Erase heading not required.)

Army Form C. 2118.

Place	Date	Hour	Summary of Events and Information	Remarks and references to Appendices
	24/4/18.	F.W.J	Very quiet day. Nothing to report.	
	25/4/18	F.W.J	Enemy artillery very active during the day & night.	
	26/4/18.	F.W.J	Divisional line withdrawn on the night 26/27th, new position of guns after withdrawal are shewn in Order No 12. Bn Hd Qrs moved from CANAL BANK to SIEGE CAMP. 1 man of 'A' Coy killed by shell fire.	[signature] Major. Comdg. No 36 Bn M.G.C.
	27/4/18	F.W.J	Bn Hd Qrs with transport & details moved from SIEGE CAMP to GRABBO CAMP. Our artillery heavily shelled WIELTJE during the day. Enemy patrol was fired on by our M.G's & dispersed. 1 man of 'B' Coy wounded.	
	28/4/18.	F.W.J	Very heavy bombardment by both sides during the day and night. 1 man of 'A' Coy. killed.	
	29/4/18	F.W.J	Very heavy shelling continued on both sides. 1 man, 'A' Coy, 2 men, 'B' Coy. wounded.	
	30/4/18.	F.W.J	The following relief took place:- 'D' Coy relieved 'B' Coy. and 'B' Coy relieved 'A' Coy in accordance with Order No 13.	

(A9475) Wt W2358/P360 600,000 12/17 D. D. & L. Sch 52a. Forms/C2118/15

S E C R E T.

Copy No....A.....

36 Battn. Machine Gun Corps Order No 3.

1. The 36th. Division will relieve the 1st. Division in the Right Brigade Sector on the night 6th 7th. April.

2. "A" Coy. 36th. Battn. Machine Gun Corps (16 guns) will relieve "B" Coy. 1st. Battn. Machine Gun Corps in the Front System.

3. "B" Coy. 36th. Battn. Machine Gun Corps (15 guns) will relieve "D" Coy. 1st. Battn. Machine Gun Corps in the Support System.

4. All gun stores will be taken into the Line with the exception of belts which will be handed over by 1st. Battn. M.G.C. to the number of 10 per gun in the Line - and equivalent number (310) will be handed over to Transport Officer 1st. Battn. M.G.C. at the Transport Camp.

5. 36th. Battn. M.G.C. will march at 1-15 p.m. 6th. April to TURCO HUTS, less "A" and "B" Coys. who will remain until 6 p.m. at the Battn. Transport Camp Brielen Cross Roads when they will proceed under direction of guides provided by 1st. Battn. M.G.C. to their several positions in the line.

6. Qr. Mr. will arrange tea for these two companies at the Transport Camp.

7. All Trench Stores, maps etc. will be taken over and receipts given, lists of such stores being forwarded to Battalion Headquarters on the 7th. April.

8. Transport Officer will arrange sufficient limbers to take "A" and "B" Coys. to the Line. These limbers will return to their Transport Camp on completion.

9. Hd. Qrs. and Coy. Qr. Mr. Stores will be taken to TURCO HUTS direct, a minimum of limbers being utilized. - They will return to Transport Camp as soon as they have off loaded.

10. Completion of relief to be reported by code word "DUN".

11. Acknowledge.

[signature]..........Lieut. & Adjt.
No 36 Battn. Machine Gun Corps.

Copy No. 1. C.O.
2. Division "Q".
3. " "G".
4. 1st. Battn. Machine Gun Corps.
5. "A" Coy.
6. "B" "
7. "C" "
8. "D" "
9. Qr. Mr.
10. Transport Officer.
11. War Diary.
12. 107th Inf. Brigade
13. File.
14. ".

S E C R E T.

Copy No...9:...

36th. Battalion Machine Gun Corps Order No 4.

1. 36th. Battalion Machine Gun Corps is responsible for the following gun positions in the Battle Zone.

(1)	C.1[illegible].b.00.[illegible]2.	1 gun.	
(2)	C.17.a.9[illegible].	1 gun.	
(3)	C.1[illegible].b.98.[illegible].	1 gun.	
(4)	C.10.b.30.2[illegible].	1 gun.	
(5)	C.17.c.[illegible].0[illegible].	1 gun.	(Cheddar Villa).
(6)	C.17.a.07.[illegible].	1 gun.	
(7)	C.10.c.9[illegible].4[illegible].	1 gun.	
(8)	C.11.a.00.[illegible].	1 gun.	(Total 8 guns).

2. The Company billetted under the present arrangements with Battn. Hdqrs. will be the Coy. to man these positions on the order being received.

3. The O's.C. the two companies out of the Line will take necessary steps to reconnoitre these positions and the routes to them as soon as possible.

4. Until full complement of guns is made up and further instructions are issued, the positions will be manned in the order named above.

5. Arrangements for Pack Animals to carry the guns to the Battle Zone will be notified later.

6. The Coy. mentioned in para 2 above is responsible that 5.000 rounds in boxes are kept in serviceable condition at each position.

....J Wilson.......Lieut. & Adjt.

No 36 Battn. Machine Gun Corps.

8th. April 1918.

Copy No. 1. O.C. "A" Coy.
2. O.C. "B" "
3. O.C. "C" "
4. O.C. "D" "
5. 36th. Division.
6. 107th. Inf. Brigade.
7. 108th. " "
8. 109th. " "
9. War Diary.
10. File.

S E C R E T.

Copy No 9

Reference Map 1/20.000.

36 Battalion Machine Gun Corps Order No 6.

1. Owing to the sudden move of "C" Coy. to another area of operations, Order No. 5. of 9th. April is hereby cancelled and the following substituted.

2. On the night of 13th/14th. April "D" Coy. will relieve "A" and "B" Coys. in the following positions.

VACHER	4 guns.	"A" Coy.	
YORK	1 gun.		
WINCHESTER	1 gun.		
BAVAROISE.	2 guns.		8 guns.
VON TIRPITZ	2 guns.	"B" Coy.	
GUIDA.	2 guns.		
TRAP.	1 gun.		
KEIRSELAR	2 guns.		7 guns.
		Total.	15 guns.

3. The teams of "B" Coy. relieved by "D" Coy. will in turn relieve remainder of "A" Coy. in the following positions.

GLOSTER	2 guns.	
POST No. 1. (Poelcappelle)	2 guns.	
NORFOLK.	2 guns.	
DELTA.	2 guns.	Total 8 guns.

4. On relief "A" Coy. will proceed to TURCO HUTS and be Coy. in reserve with Headquarters in TURCO HUTS.

5. Headquarters of "B" and "D" Coys. will be situated in TURCO CAMP.

6. Details of relief will be arranged between Coys. concerned.

7. Rations and water for 48 hours will be taken in by "D" Coy.

8. Completion of relief to be wired by "D" Coy. using the code word "BENT" and by "B" Coy. using code word "[illegible]".

9. O.C. "A" Coy. will on day following relief take steps to reconnoitre with sufficient Officers the Machine Gun emplacements in the Battle Zone, details of which can be obtained from the Orderly Room.

10. Signal communication as in previous order No. 5.

11. Acknowledge.

.......[signature]........Capt. & Adjt.

No 36 Battn. Machine Gun Corps.

10th April 1918.

Copy No. 1. 36th. Division.
2. 107th. Inf. Brigade.
3. O.C. "A" Coy.
4. O.C. "B" "
5. O.C. "C" "
6. O.C. "D" "
7. Quarter Master.
8. Transport Officer.
9. War Diary.
10. " "
11. File.
12. File.

Copy No 11

S E C R E T.

36 Battalion Machine Gun Corps Order No 7.

1. Relief Order No. 6. is cancelled.

2. "D" Coy. will occupy the positions in the Battle Zone as laid down (16 guns) by day on the 13th. April.

3. On the night 13th/14th. April personnel only of "B" Coy. will exchange positions with personnel only of "A" Coy in the following positions. Guns and stores of all kinds etc. being handed over in each case.

GENOA.	2 guns will exchange with	YORK.	1 gun.	)
		WINCHESTER	1 gun.	)
ROSE.	2 " " " "	NORFOLK.	2 guns.	
STROOMBEKE	2 " " " "	BAVAROISE.	2 guns.	
PHEASANT W	1 ")			
SLAB.	1 ") " " "	GLOSTER.	2 guns.	

The remaining gun teams of both "A" and "B" Coys. will remain as they are now situated.

4. On the night 14th/15th. all gun teams of "A" Coy. will withdraw to Battalion Headquarters - unless further orders as to their destination are issued. No gun teams to move before 7 p.m.

"B" Coy. will retain their present positions at :-

VON TIRPITZ.	2 guns.
KEERSELARE.	2 guns.
CAT POST.	2 guns.
PHEASANT E.	1 gun.
PHEASANT TR.	1 gun. Total 8 guns.

and also the positions taken over previous night from "A" Coy. Total 16 guns.

5. All details of relief to be arranged between Coys.

6. Section Headquarters will be situated as follows.

NORFOLK.	1 Officer.
HAANIXBEEK.	2 Officers.
GENOA.	1 Officer.

7. Relief as laid down in para. 3. will be reported to Capt. Moorehouse at Brigade Hdqrs. ALBERTA, and withdrawal of "A" Coy. on 14th/15th. to Battalion Headquarters.

8. Transport Officer will arrange to provide sufficient transport for the moving of "A" Coy. on the night 14/15th.

9. Pack animals at present in Forward Horse lines will move back to Battalion transport lines after "D" Coy. have taken up positions in the Battle Zone.

10. Position of Battalion Hdqrs. will be notified to all concerned later.

11. Headquarters of the Coy. manning the Battle Zone and also remaining Coys will be with Battn. Hdqrs.

12. Acknowledge.

[signature] Capt. & Adjt.

36 Battn. Machine Gun Corps.

12th. April 1918.

P.T.O.

Copy No. 1. 36th. Division.
2. 107th. Infantry Brigade.
3. 109th. Infantry Brigade.
4. O.C. "A" Coy.
5. O.C. "B" "
6. O.C. "D" "
7. Quarter Master.
8. Transport Officer.
9. War Diary.
10. " "
11. File.
12. "

S E C R E T. Copy No..11....

No 36 Battalion Machine Gun Corps Order No 8.

1. On the afternoon 15th. April "D" Coy. will take over 4 gun positions R7. 8. 9. & 11 at Weiltze and 2 gun positions M11 & 12 at Pickelhaube, now held by the 41st. Battn. M.G.C.

2. These positions will be taken up by the guns now occupying positions No 3. 4. 5. 6. 7. & 12.

3. Guides from the 41st. Battn. will be at Road junction C.22.a.50.40. at 3 p.m. 15th. April.

4. Relief to be complete by 7 p.m. and reported by Code Words "Bomb Boxes" to Battalion Headquarters.

5. List of Trench Stores taken over will be rendered to this Office by mid-day 16th. April.

6. On the night 15th/16th. April the 16 guns of "B" Coy. N. of the Steenbeek will be withdrawn to Canal Bank.

7. Details of transport for relief has been communicated direct to Coy. concerned.

8. At 12 midnight the guns from Tirpitz, York, and Winchester will be withdrawn.
At 1 a.m. guns from Keerselare and Bazazoise will be withdrawn.
At 2 a.m. guns at Pheasant East, Pheasant Trench, Cat, Norfolk and Gloster will be withdrawn.

9. Each Section when loaded up will move off independently to Canal Bank where they will be met by a guide at Bridge 4.

10. Each Section will send a N.C.O. to report to Alberta when the withdrawal of Section is complete.

11. All Signalling Equipment will be withdrawn and as much S.A.A. stores other than that already arranged for. S.A.A. which cannot be withdrawn is to be dumped in shell holes, boxes first being opened.

12. Completion of withdrawal will be reported to Battalion Hdqrs. by code words "Ammunition to-night".

13. Acknowledge.

15th April 1918

........................Capt. & Adjt.

No 36 Battn. Machine Gun Corps.

Copy No 1. 36th. Division.
2. 41st. Battn. Machine Gun Corps.
3. 107th. Inf. Bde.
4. 109th. " "
5. O.C. "A" Coy.
6. O.C. "B" "
7. O.C. "D" "
8. Quarter Master.
9. Transport Officer.
10. War Diary.
11. " "
12. File.

S E C R E T. Copy No...9....

No 36 Battalion Machine Gun Corps Order No. 9.

1. On the night of 17th/18th. April, 6 guns as under, now manned by "D" Coy. will be relieved by a similar number of guns of the 4th. Belgian Division.
   2 guns OBLONG FARM.
   2 " Boschcastel.
   2 " No 10 & 11. in C.11.a. Total 6.

2. Guides for the above guns and also the Officer from BOSCHCASTEL will report to Battalion Headquarters before 6 p.m. to-night.

3. The Machine Gun personnel of 4th. Belgian Division will arrive at Bridge 4 at 7 p.m. and will be taken up to their positions by the above mentioned guides.

4. On completion of relief personnel of "D" Coy. relieved will proceed to Trabnsport Lines Siege Camp.

5. All guns, stores. S.A.A. will be removed. Transport Officer will arrange for necessary transport required.

6. Completion of relief to be reported to Battalion Headquarters as soon as the last man has passed West of Bridge 4.

7. Acknowledge.

..J Wilson.......Capt. & Adjt.

No 36 Batt. Machine Gun Corps.

17th. April 1918.

Copy No. 1. 36th. Division.
2. 107th. Inf. Brigde.
3. 4th. Belgian Division.
4. O.C. "A" Coy.
5. O.C. "B" "
6. O.C. "D" "
7. Quarter Master.
8. Transport Officer.
9. War Diary.
10. " "
11. File.
12. "

S E C R E T. Copy No....12....

No 36 Battalion Machine Gun Corps Order No 10.

1. On the morning of 22nd. April "B" Coy. will relieve "A" Coy. in the Reserve line.

2. Details of relief to be arranged between Coys. concerned.

3. "B" Coy. will take over and man all Anti Aircraft positions held by "A" Coy.

4. Belt boxes containing Tracer Ammunition will be handed over and receipts obtained; a similar number of boxes being handed over to "A" Coy. in exchange.

5. "A" Coy. on relief will move to Canal Bank.

6. Headquarters of "A" and "B" Coys. will remain at Canal Bank.

7. Transport Officer will provide necessary transport to carry out the relief.

8. Lists of Trench Stores, Ammunition, Bombs, Tracer Ammunition etc. at each gun position will be rendered to this Office by 9 a.m. 23rd.

9. Completion of relief will be reported by Code words "RIFLE GRENADES".

10. Acknowledge.

J Wilson ....Capt. & Adjt.

No 36 Batt. Machine Gun Corps.

20th. April 1918.

Copy No 1. Commanding Officer.
2. Headquarters.
3. 36th. Div. "G".
4. " " Sigs.
5. O.C. "A" Coy.
6. O.C. "B" "
7. O.C. "C" "
8. O.C. "D" "
9. Quarter Master.
10. Transport Officer.
11. War Diary.
12. " "
13. File.
14. "
15. 107th. Inf. Bde.
16. 109th. " "

S-E C R E T. Copy No. 14

No 36 Battalion Machine Gun Corps.

PROVISIONAL INSTRUCTIONS IN THE EVENT OF AN ATTACK ON 36th DIVL. FRONT.

1. 1/ Brigade Headquarters of the Brigades holding the line will move to HILL TOP. Officers commanding companies in the line will report there as soon as possible, the Forward Coy. reporting to Right Brigade, and Support Coy. to the Left Brigade.

2. 2/ The guns of the companies East of the Canal will maintain their positions to the last.

3. 3/ In the event of a withdrawal by the Infantry the withdrawal will be covered by the Machine Guns in the line. If ultimately the Infantry take up a line on the Canal Bank, the Forward guns will cross the Canal and reform behind the West Bank.

4. 4/ In the event of neither of the Coy. Commdrs. of the Forward Coys. being available - the guns mentioned in para. 3. above will come under the orders of the Coy. Commdr. detailed for the defence of the Canal line.

5. 5/ In addition to the 3 positions on the East Bank, and the 8 on the West Bank which have already been sited - a further eight positions on the East Bank are being sited, and marked with boards bearing letters M.G. These positions will be occupied by the guns under para 3. above.

6. 6/ On the order to "Stand to" being received the Coy. at Siege Camp will be prepared to move at 5 minutes notice. The O.C. of this Coy. will report at once ~~thm~~ to Bde. Hdqrs. of the Bde. in Reserve at HOSPITAL FARM, Sheet 28 N.W.1. B.19.d.10.00. This Coy. will come under the orders of the Brigade in Reserve.

7. 7/ Details of all Coys. forward of Siege Camp and billeted at Siege Camp will move with Battalion Transport Lines.

8. 8/ All Officers and N.C.O's. of the Forward Coys. are to reconnoitre and make themselves thoroughly acquainted with the defences of the Canal Bank, paying especial attention to the positions mentioned in para 5.

9. 9/ Acknowledge.

J. Wilson.......Capt. & Adjt.

No 36 Batt. Machine Gun Corps.

21st. April 1918.

Copy No	
1.	Commanding Officer.
2.	Headquarters.
3.	O.C. "A" Coy.
4.	O.C. "B" Coy.
5.	O.C. "C" "
6.	O.C. "D" "
7.	Quarter Master.
8.	Transport Officer.
9.	36th. Division 'G'
10.	" " Sigs.
11.	107th. Inf. Brigade.
12.	108th. " "
13.	109th. " "
14.	War Diary.
15.	" "
16.	File.
17.	"

S E C R E T. Copy No..12...

No 36 Battalion Machine Gun Corps Order No 11.

---

1. The following re-organization of guns will take place as under.

2. On the night 22nd/23rd. April positions now manned by "D" Coy. will be relieved as follows.

SECRET.

ADDENDUM TO 36th BN.M.G.CORPS ORDER No 11.

Para 3, add -

2 guns of B Coy now at ENGLISH FARM will be relieved by 2 guns of A Coy.

Para 4,

For B.16.d.8.8., read C.16.d.2.8.

----------------Cppt & Adjt.

22nd April 1918. No 36 Batt Machine Gun Copps.

2 guns

guns of

y 2 guns

2 guns

Bank

5. In the event of an attack on this front and the necessity arising, the remaining 4 guns of "B" Coy. are at the disposal of 107th. Infantry Brigade for Counter attack on Muller Cot line. O.C. "B" Coy. will arrange for the Section Officer concerned to get into touch with O.C. the Counter Attack Battalion.

6. The Coy. in Reserve at SIEGE CAMP will despatch 3 Sections to occupy positions to be sited at the following localities.

4 guns at TROIS TOURS.
4 " " BRIELEN WORKS.
4 " about WAGRAM FARM defences in B.23.

The remaining Section is at the disposal of G.O.C. Reserve Bde. Bde. Hdqrs., Hospital Farm.

7. All new gun positions mentioned above will be supplied with 8000 rounds S.A.A. in bulk, and 1 box No 5 Mills Grenades per gun. Indent to be rendered to Battalion Headquarters at earliest opportunity.

8. All existing A.A. positions will be maintained.

9. O.C. Reserve Coy. at SIEGE CAMP will take necessary steps to ensure that all Section Officers and N.C.Os. acquaint themselves with the positions to be manned and routes to them.

10. Acknowledge.

J Wilson..........Capt. & Adjt.

No 36 Batt. Machine Gun Corps.

22nd. April 1918.

P.T.O.

S E C R E T.   Copy No..12....

No 36 Battalion Machine Gun Corps Order No 11.

---

1. The following re-organization of guns will take place as under.

2. On the night 22nd/23rd. April positions now manned by "D" Coy. will be relieved as follows.

2 guns at ALBERTA,	by 2 guns of "B" Coy.	
2 " " CHEDDAR VILLA	" 2 " " "A". "	
2 " " PICARDHAUSE,	" 2 " " "A". "	
4 " " WIELTJE,	" 4 " " "B". "	

3/ By day on the 23rd.
2 guns of "B" Coy. now at HICHLAND FARM will be relieved by 2 guns of "D" Coy.
2 guns of "B" Coy. now at LOON FARM will be relieved by 2 guns of "D" Coy.
2 guns of "B" Coy. now at BELLE ALLIANCE will be relieved by 2 guns of "D" Coy.
2 guns of "B" Coy. now at WILSON'S FARM will be relieved by 2 guns of "D" Coy.
Remaining 8 guns of "D" Coy. will be responsible for Canal Bank defences. 3 on East Bank, and 5 on West Bank.

4/ On the night 23rd./24th.
"B" Coy. will occupy the following positions.

CORNER COT.	2 guns.
VLAMSKELS.	2 "
B.16.d.2.8.	2 "

"A" Coy. will occupy

BUSSAERT	2 guns.
RAT FARM	2 "
VON HUGEL	2 "

5. In the event of an attack on this front and the necessity arising, the remaining 4 guns of "B" Coy. are at the disposal of 107th. Infantry Brigade for Counter attack on Julier Cot line.
O.C. "B" Coy. will arrange for the Section Officer concerned to get into touch with O.C. the Counter Attack Battalion.

6. The Coy. in Reserve at SIEGE CAMP will despatch 3 Sections to occupy positions to be sited at the following localities.
4 guns at TROIS TOURS.
4 " " BRIELEN WORKS.
4 " About WAGRAM FARM defences in B.23.
The remaining Section is at the disposal of G.O.C. Reserve Bde. Bde. Hdqrs., Hospital Farm.

7. All new gun positions mentioned above will be supplied with 3000 rounds S.A.A. in bulk, and 1 box No 5 Mills Grenades per gun. Indent to be rendered to Battalion Headquarters at earliest opportunity.

8. All existing A.A. positions will be maintained.

9. O.C. Reserve Coy. at SIEGE CAMP will take necessary steps to ensure that all Section Officers and N.C.Os. acquaint themselves with the positions to be manned and routes to them.

10. Acknowledge.

J Wilson ....Capt. & Adjt.

No 36 Batt. Machine Gun Corps.

22nd. April 1918.

P.T.O.

Copy No 1. Commanding Officer.
2. O.C. "A" Coy.
3. O.C. "B" "
4. O.C. "C" "
5. O.C. "D" "
6. Quarter Master.
7. Transport Officer.
8. 36th. Division.
9. 107th. Inf. Brig'e.
10. 108th. " "
11. 109th. " "
12. War Diary.
13. " "
14. File.

S E C R E T.

Copy No....6.......

No 36 Battalion Machine Gun Corps Order No 12.

1. The Line will be withdrawn to-night 26th/27th April, to a new line with Outposts on Calliban Trench line, and the Canal as the main line of resistance.

2. The following guns of "A" Coy. will be withdrawn, and will occupy new positions as under.

WITHDRAWN.	OCCUPY.
Chedder Villa.	Wilsons Farm.
Bossairt. Rat. Von Hugel.	6 guns Canal Bank. 2 East. 4 West.

3. The following guns of "B" Coy. will be withdrawn and occupy new positions as under.

WITHDRAWN.	OCCUPY.
Alberta.	Belle Alliance.
Corner.Cot.	Foch.
Van Heule.	Highland.
	4 guns Canal Bank. 1 East. 3 West.

4. The guns of "D" Coy. relieved in Farms. 2. and 3. together with the 3 guns now in reserve at Canal Bank, will proceed to Siege Camp.

5. Limbers have been arranged to carry out the withdrawal.

6. Headquarters of "A" and "B" Coys. will remain with 109th. and 107th. Infantry Brigades respectively at Canal Bank.

7. Battn. Hdqrs. and Hdqrs. of "C" and "D" Coys. will be at Siege Camp.

8. As much S.A.A. etc. will be brought from the evacuated positions as possible.

9. Completion of withdrawal will be reported to Battn. Hdqrs. by the Code words "RUM RATION".

10. O.C. "D" Coy. will arrange to reconnoitre the Brielen Defences with Officersand N.C.Os. to-morrow morning at dawn.

11. O.C. "C" Coy. will provide an Officer to guide this party.

12. O.C. "C" Coy. will arrange to reconnoitre Green and Yellow Lines with 1 Officer and 1 N.C.O. per Section, and 1 man from each Gun team, as soon after dawn as possible.

13. Acknowledge.

...........Capt. & Adjt.
No 36 Battn. Machine Gun Corps.

26th. April 1918.

Copy No 1. Commanding Officer.
2. O.C. "A" Coy.
3. O.C. "B" "
4. O.C. "C" "
5. O.C. "D" "
6. War Diary.
7. File.

S E C R E T. Copy No...13....

No 36 Battalion Machine Gun Corps Order No 13.

The following Relief will take place by day on the 30th. April, unless orders to the contrary are issued.

1. "D" Coy. will relieve "C" Coy. as under,

Border Camp.	4 guns.
Brielon.	4 "
Trois Tours.	4 "
[illegible] Jn. ([illegible])	4 "

2 of the above Sections of "C" Coy. thus relieved will relieve 8 guns of "A" Coy. on Canal Bank and Wilson's Farm, these guns on relief returning at once by March Route to Battalion Headquarters, and will hold themselves in readiness to occupy the YELLOW LINE. The above portion of the relief to be complete by 12 a.m. 30th. April. O.C. "D" Coy. will leave behind at Battn. Hdqrs. sufficient guides for this purpose.

2. On the night of 30th April/1st. May, the remainder of "C" Coy. will relieve the remainder of "A" Coy.

English Farm.	2 guns.
[illegible]	4 "
Pickelhaube.	2 "

3. The personnel of "A" Coy. not returning by March Route will return to Battn. Hdqrs. by train, time and place of entrainment being notified later. They will hold themselves in readiness to man the positions in the BLUE LINE, "D" Coy. leaving behind guides for this purpose.

4. All details of relief will be arranged between Os.C. Coys. concerned.

5. Transport Officer will arrange the necessary transport to carry out the relief.

6. All Trench Stores, A.A. Sights, and Tracer Ammunition will be handed over, lists of trench stores at each position taken over being rendered to this Office by 6 p.m. on 1st. May.

7. Completion of relief will be reported by Code Words "YESTERDAY MORNING".

8. Acknowledge.

.......................Capt. & Adjt.
No 36 Battn. Machine Gun Corps.

28th. April 1918.

Copy No 1. Commanding Officer.
2. O.C. "A" Coy.
3. O.C. "B" "
4. O.C. "C" "
5. O.C. "D" "
6. Quarter Master.
7. Transport Officer.
8. 36th. Division.
9. 107th. Inf. Brigade.
10. 108th. " "
11. 109th. " "
12. War Diary.
13. " "
14. File.

May 1918

Instructions regarding War Diaries and Intelligence Summaries are contained in F. S. Regs., Part II. and the Staff Manual respectively. Title pages will be prepared in manuscript.

WAR DIARY
or
~~INTELLIGENCE SUMMARY.~~
(Erase heading not required.)

36 Bn M. G. Corps

Army Form C. 2118.

Vol 4

Place	Date	Hour	Summary of Events and Information	Remarks and references to Appendices
	May 1st.	F.W.J.	"B" "C" and "D" Coys. in the line and "A" Coy. in reserve. Artillery normal on both sides. Our M.Guns fired 4.000 rounds on various enemy positions.	
	2nd.	F.W.J.	Several of our gun positions shelled during the day but no casualties occurred. Our Machine Guns fired 4.000 rounds during the night.	
	3rd.	F.W.J.	Very heavy shelling by both sides throughout the day and night. No casualties. Our guns fired 10.000 rounds during the day and night on various targets. Small parties of the enemy were seen to be dispersed by their fire.	
	4th.	F.W.J.	Much quieter day. Our guns again fired 10.000 rounds. The following N.C.O's. and men were awarded the Military Medal. Sergts. J. Fitzsimmons, T. Owen, and J. Greer. Ptes. F.J. Peet, and E. Appleby.	
	5th.	F.W.J.	Our back areas received a little attention from enemy's guns during the day, otherwise very quiet on both sides. Our M.Gs. fired 5.000 rounds on roads and tracks behind the enemy's lines.	
	6th.	F.W.J.	Several of our gun positions were shelled during the day. No casualties. 7.000 rounds were fired by our M.Guns on selected targets. The following Officers reported from Base and were posted to Coys. as follows, Lieut. F.L. Granfield to "B" Coy. Lieut. A.J.Smyth and 2nd. Lt. R.L.Exshaw to "C" Coy.	
	7th.	F.W.J.	Artillery on both sides very quiet. Our Machine Guns fired 10.000 rounds during the night.	
	8th.	F.W.J.	"A" Coy. relieved "D" Coy. in the Brielen Defences. "D" Coy. relieved "B" Coy. in the left forward system in the line in accordance with Order No 14.	
	9th.	F.W.J.	Artillery carried out usual harassing fire. 5.000 rounds fired by our M. Guns on various targets. Sergt. T. Hume awarded the Military Medal.	
	10th.	F.W.J.	Unusually quiet day. Our M. Guns fired 5.000 rounds during the night. "D" Coy. relieved 8 guns of "C" Coy. and "A" Coy. relieved 2 guns of "C" Coy. 12 guns withdrawn. On completion of relief "C" Coy. relieved 12 guns of the 41st. Battn. M.G.C. as laid down in Order No 15.	
	11th.	F.W.J.	Quiet during the day, harassing fire carried out by both sides during the night. Our M. Guns fired 5.000 rounds on selected targets during the night.	
	12th.	F.W.J.	Very little action on either side during the day. Artillery rather ~~xxxxxx~~ lively throughout the night. Our M. Guns fired 4.000 rounds.	
	13th.	F.W.J.	Artillery action on both sides much the same as previous day, Our guns fired 4.000 rounds on various targets.	
	14th.	F.W.J.	Quiet during the day but increased activity during the night. 5 men of "C" Coy. gassed and one man wounded.	

A5834 Wt. W4973/M687 750,000 8/16 D. D. & L. Ltd. Forms/C.2118/13.

Instructions regarding War Diaries and Intelligence Summaries are contained in F. S. Regs., Part II. and the Staff Manual respectively. Title pages will be prepared in manuscript.

WAR DIARY

or

~~INTELLIGENCE SUMMARY.~~

(Erase heading not required.)

Army Form C. 2118.

Place	Date	Hour	Summary of Events and Information	Remarks and references to Appendices
	May 15th.	FWJ	Our Artillery very active during the 24 hours. Enemy's guns very quiet.	
	16th.	FWJ	Increased activity during the day and night on both sides. Our guns fired 2.000 rounds during the night. During the day "B" Coy. relieved "A" Coy. in the Brielen Defences and during the night "A" Coy. relieved "C" Coy. in the forward system as laid down in Order No 16.	
	17th.	FWJ	Quiet during the day, active during the night. Our guns fired 7.000 rounds during the night. Capt. Kitchen and Lieut. Evans "B" Coy. awarded the Military Cross. C.S.M. Carpenter "A" Coy. awarded the D.C.M.	
	18th.	FWJ	Artillery on both sides very quiet. Our guns fired 2.000 rounds on selected targets.	
	19th.	FWJ	Our Artillery carried out counter preparations during the day. Enemy guns very active during the night.	
	20th.	FWJ	Very heavy artillery action on both sides during the day and night. One man of "B" Coy. wounded.	
	21st.	FWJ	Much quieter than usual. Nothing to report.	
	22nd.	FWJ	During the 24 hours our guns shelled enemy lines at intervals. Enemy guns very active on our back areas. Capt. R.B.S. Munn "C" Coy. and Lieut. L.G. Bolton late "A" Coy. awarded the M.C. Sergt. Stubbings and Pte Gilmore "A" Coy. awarded the D.C.M.	
	23rd.	FWJ	The usual artillery activity on both sides. Our Machine Guns were quiet except for A.A. work. One man of "B" Coy. wounded.	
	24th.	FWJ	Our field guns were very active on enemy front system during the day, the enemy paying special attention to back areas. At 1-30 a.m. the enemy attempted a raid on WEILTJE without success. Inter-Company relief was carried out as laid down in Order No 17.	
	25th.	FWJ	Usual harassing fire throughout the day and night. Trench Mortars were rather active for a short period on our front gun positions, no casualties occurred.	
	26th.	FWJ	Artillery on both sides very quiet. Our M. Guns fired 4.000 rounds on selected targets. Enemy M. Guns more active than usual.	
	27th.	FWJ	Our artillery of all calibres very active along the whole of the front. Enemy much quieter than usual. Our M.Gs. fired 9.500 rounds on various targets.	
	28th.	FWJ	Our guns very active throughout the day and night. Enemy's artillery unusually active through the day. Our M.Gs. fired [illegible].000 rounds on selected targets.	
	29th.	FWJ	Our field guns made some very effective shooting on the enemy front line. Enemy guns were very active on our forward and back areas, using a large number of gas shells.	
	30th.	FWJ	Both sides much quieter than usual. 4.000 rounds were fired by our M. Guns during the night. An enemy plane brought down by our Maching Guns.	
	31st.	FWJ	The usual counter battery work on both sides. Our M. Guns fired [illegible].000 rounds at selected targets during the night. Battalion Headquarters shelled, 3 men killed and 2 wounded.	Comndg 3rd Bn. [illegible] Major

A5834 Wt. W4973/M687 750,000 8/16 D. D. & L. Ltd. Forms/C.2118/13.

SECRET. Copy No..13....

No 36 Battalion Machine Gun Corps Order No 14.

1. On the morning 8th. May "A" Coy. will relieve "D" Coy. in the Brielen Defences.

2. When relieved "D" Coy. will relieve "B" Coy. in the Left Sector, Forward System, of the Line.

3. "D" Coy. will arrange to take over 2 tripods, and 12 belt boxes per gun at "Wind up" positions, to allow these positions to be relieved by day.

4. Range Cards and details of S.O.S. Lines will be handed over.

5. All A.A. gun positions will be taken over and manned.

6. Details of relief will be arranged by Coy. Comdrs. concerned.

7. Transport Officer will arrange necessary transport to carry out relief.

8. On relief "B" Coy. will return to Battn. Hdqrs. Camp by March Route.

9. Hdqrs. of "A" Coy. will be at Border Camp.

10. RECONNAISANCE.
O.C. "D" Coy. will arrange that all Officers reconnoitre forward positions before relief.
O.C. "A" Coy. will arrange that all Officers reconnoitre Brielen Defences, before relief.
O.C. "B" Coy. will arrange for 1 Officer per Section to reconnoitre Green and Yellow Lines before relief.

11. Lists of Trench Stores, A.A. Sights, Tracer Ammunition etc., taken over, will be rendered to this Office by 6 p.m. on 9th. March.

12. Completion of relief will be reported by Code words "ARRIVE[illegible] TO-DAY".

13. Acknowledge.

......................Capt. & Adjt.
No 36 Batt. Machine Gun Corps.

4th. May 1918.

Copy No 1. Commanding Officer.
2. O.C. "A" Coy.
3. O.C. "B" "
4. O.C. "C" "
5. O.C. "D" "
6. Quarter Master.
7. Transport Officer.
8. 36th. Division.
9. 107th. Inf. Brigade.
10. 108th. " "
11. 109th. " "
12. War Diary.
13. " "
14. File.

S E C R E T.   Copy No.....15.....

No 36 Battalion Machine Gun Corps Order No 15.

1. In conjunction with 36th. Division Order No 195, the following re-organization of Machine Gun dispositions in the line will take place on night of 10th/11th. May.

2. The following guns will be withdrawn.

Highland Farm.	2.
Foch Farm.	2.
Canadian Farm.	2.
Hampshire Farm.	2.
Canal Bank (C.25.a.60.40.)	
(C.25.a.90.40.)	2.
Pioneer Farm.	2.

3. "D" Coy. will relieve "C" Coy. as under.

Wilson's Farm.	2.
Cross Roads Farm.	2.
Pickelhaube.	2.
Canal Bank (C.25.d.00.80.)	
(C.25.d.45.40.)	2.

4. The two guns of "A" Coy. withdrawn from Pioneer Farm will relieve the two guns of "C" Coy. on the Canal Bank at
C.19.c.38.18.
C.25.a.40.80.
and on completion of relief come under the orders of "D" Coy.

5. Details of relief to be arranged between Os.C. "C" and "D" Coys. 36th. Battn. M.G.C.

6. On completion of above relief "C" Coy. will relieve 6 guns of "A" Coy. 41st. Battn. M.G.C. in the forward area as under
Nos. F6. F7. F11. F13. and F28. (2 guns)
and 6 guns of "D" Coy. 41st. Battn. M.G.C. as under
Nos. 9. 10. 11. 12. 13. and 15. in the Kaaie Defences.
This latter part of the relief may be completed in daylight.

7. 41st. Battn. M.G.C. will leave in one man per gun position until night of 11th/12th May.

8. Details as to guides etc. will be arranged between O.C. "C" Coy. 36th. Battn. M.G.C. and the two Coy. Comdrs. concerned of 41st. Battn. M.G.C.

9. All A.A. positions, S.O.S. and Barrage Lines will be taken over.

10. Lists of Trench Stores etc. taken over will be rendered to this Office by 6 p.m. 13th. inst.

11. Completion of relief to be reported by O.C. "C" Coy. by the Code words "TEN MAPS".

12. Acknowledge.

..................Capt. & Adjt.

No 36 Battn. Machine Gun Corps.

10th. May 1918.

P.T.O.

Copy No	1.	Commanding Officer.
	2.	O.C. "A" Coy.
	3.	O.C. "B" "
	4.	O.C. "C" "
	5.	O.C. "D" "
	6.	Quarter Master.
	7.	Transport Officer.
	8.	36th. Division.
	9.	107th. Inf. Brigade.
	10.	108th. " "
	11.	109th. " "
	12.	41st. Battn. M.G.C.
	13.	4th. Belgian Division.
	14.	War Diary.
	15.	" "
	16.	File.

S E C R E T. Copy No......13...

No 36 Battalion Machine Gun Corps Order No 16.

1. On the morning 16th. May "B" Coy. will relieve 14 guns of "A" Coy. in the Brielen Defences and 2 guns on Canal Bank.

2. The 2 guns (of "B" Coy) on Canal Bank will come under the tactical command of "D" Coy.

3. On relief "A" Coy. will relieve 8 guns of "C" Coy. in the right sector forward system; 2 at English Farm and 6 in the Kasie Salient.

4. These teams when relieved will proceed by march route to X camp.

5. On the night 16th/17th May "A" Coy. will relieve the remaining 8 guns of "C" Coy. in the forward system.

6. The personnel of these 8 teams will entrain for X camp. Time and place will be notified later.

7. All details of relief will be arranged between Company Commanders concerned.

8. Transport Officer will arrange for necessary transport to complete relief.

9. All Trench Stores, A.A. Sights, Range Cards, and Barrage Lines etc., will be handed over, and lists rendered to this Office by 12 noon 18th. inst.

10. RECONNAISSANCE BEFORE RELIEF.
O.C. "A" Coy. will arrange for all Officers to reconnoitre as far as possible, positions now held by "C" Coy.
O.C. "B" Coy. will arrange for all Officers to reconnoitre Brielen Defences.
O.C. "C" Coy. will arrange for all Officers to reconnoitre the Green, Blue and Yellow Lines.

11. Completion of relief will be reported by the Code words "TRACER AMMUNITION."

12. Acknowledge.

13/5/18

..................Capt. & Adjt.
No 36 Batt. Machine Gun Corps.

Copy No 1. Commanding Officer.
2. O.C. "A" Coy.
3. O.C. "B" "
4. O.C. "C" "
5. O.C. "D" "
6. Quarter Master.
7. Transport Officer.
8. Signal Officer.
9. 36th. Division.
10. 107th. Inf. Brigade.
11. 108th. " "
12. 109th. " "
13. War Diary.
14. " "
15. File.

S E C R E T.   Copy No........

No 36 Battn. Machine Gun Corps Order No 17.

1. On the morning 24th. May, "C" Coy. will relieve 14 guns of "B" Coy. in the Brielen Defences and 2 guns on Canal Bank. On relief these 2 guns will come under the tactical command of "D" Coy.

2. On relief "B" Coy. will relieve 4 guns of "D" Coy. on Canal Bank.

3. These teams when relieved will proceed by March Route to X Camp.

4. On the night 24th/25th "B" Coy. will relieve the remaining 12 guns of "D" Coy. in the Left Sector Forward System.

5. The personnel of these 12 teams will entrain for X Camp. Time and place will be notified later.

6. All details of reliefs to be arranged between Company Commanders concerned.

7. Transport Officer will arrange for necessary transport to complete reliefs.

8. All Trench Stores, Range Cards and Barrage Lines etc. will be handed over and lists rendered to Battn. Orderly Room by 12 noon 26th. May. A.A. sights will not be handed over.

9. O.C. "B" Coy. will arrange for all Officers to reconnoitre as far as possible, positions now held by "D" Coy.
O.C. "C" Coy. will arrange for all Officers to reconnoitre the Brielen Defences.
O.C. "D" Coy. will arrange for a proportion of Officers & N.C.Os. to reconnoitre the Green, Blue and Yellow Lines.

10. O.C. "B" Coy. will send one man to each position East of Canal on night 23rd/24th, who will remain in these positions.

11. Completion of relief will be reported by Code word "FINE COPY".

12. Acknowledge.

J. Wilson ....Capt. & Adjt.
No 36 Batt. Machine Gun Corps.

21st. May 1918.

Copy No 1.		Commanding Officer.
2.		O.C. "A" Coy.
3.		O.C. "B" "
4.		O.C. "C" "
5.		O.C. "D" "
6.		Quarter Master.
7.		Transport Officer.
8.		Signal Officer.
9.		36th. Division.
10.		107th. Inf. Brigade.
11.		108th. " "
12.		109th. " "
13.		War Diary.
14.		" "
15.		File.

Instructions regarding War Diaries and Intelligence Summaries are contained in F. S. Regs., Part II, and the Staff Manual respectively. Title pages will be prepared in manuscript.

WAR DIARY
or
~~INTELLIGENCE SUMMARY.~~
(Erase heading not required.)

36th M. G. Battn.

Army Form C. 2118.

Vol 5

Place	Date	Hour	Summary of Events and Information	Remarks and references to Appendices
	June 1st	Hof	Distribution of Coys were as follows. 'A' & 'B' Coys in the Front System, 'C' Coy in the Brielen Defences & 'D' Coy in Divisional Reserve. During the day 'D' Coy relieved 'C' Coy & at night 'C' Coy relieved 'A' Coy who on relief came into Divisional Reserve. This relief was carried out as laid down in Order No 18.	
	June 2nd	Hof	Nothing unusual occured. Artillery on both sides normal. Our machine guns fired 10,000 rounds during the day & night on various enemy positions & aircraft.	
	June 3rd	Hof	Much the same as yesterday. Our M. Guns fired 5,000 rounds.	
	June 4th	Hof	Increased activity both with artillery & Aircraft all day. Our M Guns fired 12,000 rounds on selected targets & aircraft.	

(A9175) Wt W2358/P360 600,000 12/17 D. D. & L. Sch. 52a. Forms/C2118/15

Army Form C. 2118.

Instructions regarding War Diaries and Intelligence Summaries are contained in F. S. Regs., Part II. and the Staff Manual respectively. Title pages will be prepared in manuscript.

WAR DIARY
or
~~INTELLIGENCE SUMMARY.~~
(Erase heading not required.)

Place	Date	Hour	Summary of Events and Information	Remarks and references to Appendices
	5th June		On the night 4th/5th 'B' & 'C' Coys were ~~&~~ relieved by Belgian Machine Gun Coys. During the day 'D' Coy were also relieved by a Belgian M. G. Coy. All companies on relief proceeded to TUNNELLING CAMP. 'A' Coy & Battn Headquarters from GRABBS CAMP joined the remainder of the Battn. The relief & moves were carried out in accordance with Order No 19.	
	6th June		The Battalion in TUNNELLING CAMP. All guns & Equipment throughly cleaned.	
	7th June		The C.O held a conference with Coy Commdrs & decided what method of training to adopt while the Battn is out of the line.	
	8th June		Training as per programme.	
	9th June		Church Parade.	

(A9175) Wt W2358/P360 600,000 12/17 D. D. & L. Sch 52a. Forms/C2118/15

Instructions regarding War Diaries and Intelligence Summaries are contained in F. S. Regs., Part II. and the Staff Manual respectively. Title pages will be prepared in manuscript.

WAR DIARY
or
~~INTELLIGENCE SUMMARY~~.
(*Erase heading not required.*)

Army Form C. 2118.

Place	Date	Hour	Summary of Events and Information	Remarks and references to Appendices
	10th June 11th June 12th June 13th June 14th June 15th June	F.W.J.	Training as per programme.	
	16th June	F.W.J.	Church Parades.	
	17th June	F.W.J.	Battalion Sports.	
	18th June 19th June 20th June 21st June 22nd June	F.W.J.	Training as per programme.	

(A9175) Wt W2358/P360 6c0,000 12/7 D. D. & L. Sch 52a. Forms/C2118/15

Instructions regarding War Diaries and Intelligence Summaries are contained in F. S. Regs., Part II, and the Staff Manual respectively. Title pages will be prepared in manuscript.

WAR DIARY
or
~~INTELLIGENCE SUMMARY~~.
(Erase heading not required.)

Army Form C. 2118.

Place	Date	Hour	Summary of Events and Information	Remarks and references to Appendices
	23rd June	Kof	Training as per programme	
	24th June	Kof	do	
	25 June	JW.	A + B Coys proceeded to Cormette for range practice. Personnel by train transport by march route. B Coy recalled from Cormette at 2 P.M. C + D Coys. training as per programme.	
	26th	JW.	B. Coy arrived from Cormette. A Coy firing at Cormette C + D Coy training as per programme.	
	27th	JW.	Coys training as per programme.	
	28th	JW.	Coys training as per programme	
	29th	JW.	Coys training as per programme. Advance party from B Coy left for Cormette. Move of B Coy to Cormette cancelled. 10 P.M. Great increase in enemy night flying. No bombs dropped anywhere near camp	

(A9175) Wt. W2358/P369 600,000 12/17 D. D. & L. Sch. 52a. Forms/C2118/15.

Instructions regarding War Diaries and Intelligence Summaries are contained in F. S. Regs., Part II, and the Staff Manual respectively. Title pages will be prepared in manuscript.

WAR DIARY
or
~~INTELLIGENCE SUMMARY~~.
(Erase heading not required.)

Army Form C. 2118.

Place	Date	Hour	Summary of Events and Information	Remarks and references to Appendices
Field	30th	do	Church Parades. A Coy. arrived back from [illegible]. Several E.A. flying at a great height by day. Great enemy aerial activity by night.	

[illegible signature]
Lt. Colonel.
Comdg. 36 Bn. M. G. Corps.

(A9175) Wt W2358/P360 600,000 12/.7 D. D. & L. Sch 52a. Forms/C2118/15

36th Bn Machine Gun Corps.

Instructions regarding War Diaries and Intelligence Summaries are contained in F. S. Regs., Part II. and the Staff Manual respectively. Title pages will be prepared in manuscript.

WAR DIARY
~~or~~
~~INTELLIGENCE SUMMARY.~~
(*Erase heading not required.*)

July 1918.

Army Form C. 2118.

Vol 6

Place	Date	Hour	Summary of Events and Information	Remarks and references to Appendices
On Service.	1.		Divisional Horse Show held at Aerodrome, PROVEN. Training finished at 10 a.m. Warning Order for move to new area received.	
	2.		Coys training according to the Training Programme. Orders received for move to XVI French Corps Reserve Area.	
	3.		Battalion moved by march route to EECKE with 108th Inf. Bde. Group of units. Officers of A, B & C Coys reconnoitred XVI French Corps Reserve Line under the guidance of Officers and N.C.O's left behind by 168th French Infantry Division.	
	4.		Reconnaisance continued.	
	5.		Reconnaisance by Officers and N.C.O's of the sector of the front system held by the 41st French Division commenced. Details for the relief of that Division arranged.	
	6. 7.		Reliefs carried out in accordance with 36th Bn Machine Gun Corps Order No 21 attached. Battn. Advanced Headquarters opened at (Sheet 27 S.E.) Q.13.d.35.55. Rear Headquarters and Transport Lines remain at EECKE.	
	8.		Quiet day. Heavy thunderstorm in the evening.	
	9.		Very clear day. Great aerial activity on our part. Enemy shelled trenches in front of FONTAINE HOUCK.	
	10.		Showery day. Battalion Headquarters shelled with heavy H.E. shrapnel. 'A' Coy Hd. Qrs. in the line shelled with 5.9 with instantaneous fuses. BAILLEUL shelled intermittently during the day.	
	11.		Fairly quiet day. Enemy M.G's traversed our front system. Our artillery fired on BAILLEUL during the day.	
	12.		Enemy M.G's again active on front and support systems. Our artillery fired smoke shells on enemy lines opposite BAILLEUL at dawn. Enemy artillery active on roads, etc. in rear areas. 1 O.R. D Coy wounded in the Left Sector.	
			Continued -	

A5834 Wt. W4973/M687 750,000 8/16 D. D. & L. Ltd. Forms/C.2118/13.

Instructions regarding War Diaries and Intelligence Summaries are contained in F. S. Regs., Part II. and the Staff Manual respectively. Title pages will be prepared in manuscript.

WAR DIARY
or
~~INTELLIGENCE SUMMARY.~~

(*Erase heading not required.*)

Army Form C. 2118.

Place	Date	Hour	Summary of Events and Information	Remarks and references to Appendices
On Service.	13.		Normal day. Our artillery active on BALLIEUL during the day. Enemy observation balloon brought down in direction of KEMMEL.	
	14.		Enemy shelled FONTAINE HOUCK Cross Roads and KOPJE Farm with heavy H.E. Our Machine Guns fired 1,000 rds on squares X.17.b.and 18.a.during the night.	
	15.		FONTAINE HOUCK and KOPJE Farm again shelled with H.E. From 7.30 to 9.30 p.m.a large number of E.A.patrolled behind enemy lines. 4 Officers and 20 O.R.from 30th American Division attached until 19th inst for instruction.	
	16.		C Coy withdrawn from Army Line (afterwards known as Second Position) One Section mans positions ~~xxxx~~ for defence of Mt NOIR,one Section in Reserve to Left Bgde. These two sections,with the Coy. already in the Sector,form the'Left Group'under the Coy.Commander in that sector. The remaining two sections in C Coy moved to PIEBROUCK in reserve to Right Brigade. They,together with the Coy. in the Right Sector form the 'Right Group'under O.C.Right Coy. Both groups have an O.C.Forward Guns and O.C.Rear Guns in addition to the Section Commanders. Machine Guns fired on S.O.S.Lines when signal went on Left Sector Front. Enemy artillery active.	
	17.		2nd Lt F.E.C.GRANTHAM wounded. 2 O.R.wounded. Much enemy shelling in a promiscious way. M.C's fired 300 rds on E.A.	
	18.		Artillery on both sides very active. Enemy M.G'S active at night. A number of fires seen in BALLIEUL during the night.	
	19.		M.G's fired 33,000 rds in connection with the attack of the 6th Division on METEREN. Our support line shelled at 1.45 p.m.with shell gas.	
	20.		Enemy shelled front system with mustard gas. Respirators were worn for 25 minutes. M.G's fired 2000 rds on MURAL Farm,tracks in X.17.b.and APPETITE Farm. 1200 rds fired on Squares S.9.a. S.8.b. 1 O.R.wounded.	
	21.		B Coy relieved D Coy in the left group on night 21/22nd. M.G's fired 2000 rds on MURAL Farm, tracks in X.17.b.and APPETITE Farm. 4 O.R. B Coy wounded.	

Continued -

A5834 Wt. W4973/M687 750,000 8/16 D. D. & L. Ltd. Forms/C.2118/13.

Army Form C. 2118.

Instructions regarding War Diaries and Intelligence Summaries are contained in F. S. Regs., Part II. and the Staff Manual respectively. Title pages will be prepared in manuscript.

WAR DIARY
or
~~INTELLIGENCE SUMMARY~~.

(*Erase heading not required.*)

Place	Date	Hour	Summary of Events and Information	Remarks and references to Appendices
Onn Service.	22.		M.G's fired 4000 rds on roads and tracks in S.8.a.00.00.and from S.8.c.05.78 to S.14.a.25.78. Sand Quarry at M.20.b.shelled heavily,150 shells including gas shells falling between 10 and 11.15 p.m.	
	23.		M.G's fired 4000 rds on roads and tracks behind enemy lines. Enemy M.G.activity less than usual.	
	24.		M.G's fired 6000 rds on tracks,etc,behind enemy lines. 2 O.R.wounded (1 Gas)	
	25.		M.G's fired 3000 rds on tracks,cross roads,etc.behind enemy lines. Usual night shelling from the enemy. 2 O.R.wounded (Gas)	
	26.		2500 rds fired on roads and tracks as usual. Enemy artillery very active. C Coy relieved A Coy in the Right Sector of the line. 1 O.R.wounded (Gas)	
	27.		M.G's fired 10,000 rds on MURAL Farm and roads and tracks in vicinity. Lieut C.LEAVER joined from Base Depot for duty.	
	28.		M.G's fired 10,000 rds on MURAL Farm and vicinity.	
	29.		M.G's fired 6000 rds on a Battn Hd.Qrs.and roads and tracks in the vicinity.	
	30.		B Coy fired 15,000 rds on roads and tracks in view of a possible enemy relief.	
	31.		M.G's fired 3000 rds on enemy roads,etc. Heavy enemy fire during the night.	
			A.how? Major for ----------------------Lt-Colonel. 2nd August 1918. Comdg 30th Bn Machine Gun Corps.	

D. D. & L., London, E.C.
(A8004) Wt. W1771/M2031 750,000 5/17 Sch. 52 Forms/C2118/14

SECRET. Copy No..14.

No 36 Battalion Machine Gun Corps Order No 21.

1. On the nights 6th/7th. and 7th/8th. July 1918, the 36th. Battn. Machine Gun Corps will relieve the Machine Guns of the 41st. Division as under.

2. On the night 6th/7th. "A" Coy. will relieve certain guns of No. 1 Battn. of 128th. Regiment, and No 1 Battn. of 42nd. Regiment. "D" Coy. will relieve certain guns of No 1. Battn. (Front Line) of 23rd. Regiment.

3. On the night 7th/8th. July "A" Coy. will relieve certain guns of No 3 Battn. of 128th. Regiment.
"C" Coy. will relieve certain guns of No 3 Battn. of 23rd. Regiment, and No 3 Battn. of 42nd. Regiment.
"B" Coy. will relieve certain guns of No 2 Battn. of 23rd. Regiment, No 2 Battn. of 42nd. Regiment, and No 2 Battn. of 128th. Regiment.

4. The French guns are grouped in pairs so each selected positions will be relieved by a Sub Section.

5. Guides will be provided by the French for each pair of guns and will meet incoming Sections at Le Rossignol R.20.d. 75.90. at 10 p.m.

6. Each group of two guns should be numbered by the letter of the Coy. A1. A2. B1. B2. etc., and a similar arrangements made with the French guides.

7. No cooking by day is allowed in front of Mont de Cats.

8. <u>S.A.A.</u>
12 single belt boxes per gun will be taken into the line.
On the night 6th/7th, "D" Coy. will arrange to form two dumps each of 50.000 rounds at R.29.d.20.90. (Pinnace Cottage) and R.35.c.60.90.
On the same night, "A" Coy. will form a dump of 100.000 rounds at Berthen.
Two men per Limber will accompany convoy as off loaders.
The Transport Officers of "A" and "D" Coys. will accompany their respective convoys.
Coys. in the line will draw on these dumps to form a reserve at each gun position. The remaining boxes required to bring the reserve per gun up to 8.000 rounds will be drawn from Battn. HQrs. on subsequent nights.

9. No troops will cross the railway at Godewaersvelde before 9 p.m. each night.

10. Completion of relief will be reported by the code word "DEMAIN".

11. Acknowledge.

J Wilson ....Capt. & Adjt.

No 36 Batt. Machine Gun Corps.

6th. July 1918.

P.T.O.

Copy No 1. Commanding Officer.
2. O.C. "A" Coy.
3. O.C. "B" "
4. O.C. "C" "
5. O.C. "D" "
6. Quarter Master.
7. Transport Officer.
8. Signal Officer.
9. 36th. Division.
10. 107th. Inf. Brigade.
11. 108th. " "
12. 109th. " "
13. War Diary.
14. " "
15. File.

No 36 Battalion Machine Gun Corps Order No 40.

1 - The 36th. Battalion [illegible] will move by March Route on 3rd. July to the [illegible].
Route :- St. Jan ter [illegible], K.[illegible], K.[illegible], Steenvoorde (Sheet 27).

2 - Order of March, Headquarters, 'A', 'B', 'C', and 'D' Coys.
Coy. Transport will march [illegible] their respective Coys. Headquarter Transport will march with Headquarters.

3 - Head of the column will be at end of track leading from Camp to St. Jan ter Biezen at L.[illegible] at 9-45 a.m., to pass starting point at 10 a.m.

4 - Intervals as follows will be observed.
Head of the column, 300 yds from 122 Field Coy. R.E.
100 yds. between Hdqr. personnel and Hdqr. Transport.
[illegible] yds. between end of Hdqr. Transport and leading Coy.
100 yds. between end of Coy. and its own Transport.
25 yds. between every six vehicles.
100 yds. between end of leading Coy. Transport and head of next Company.

5 - Halts will be observed at [illegible] minutes to the clock hour without orders if necessary.

6 - No smoking will be allowed before the first halt.

7 - The attention of all Officers is drawn to Infantry Training Sec. [illegible] page [illegible] - 116 Field Service Regs. part 1, Chap.[illegible], 'Marches'.

8 - Acknowledge.

J Wilson
................Capt. & Adjt.
No 36 Batt. Machine Gun Corps.

2nd. July 1918.

Copy No 1. Commanding Officer, [illegible]
2. O.C. A Coy.
3. O.C. B Coy.
4. O.C. C Coy.
5. O.C. D Coy.
6. Quarter Master.
7. Transport Officer.
8. 108th. Inf. Brigade.
9. War Diary.
10. do.
11. File.

36th Battalion Machine Gun Corps. August 1918. Army Form C. 2118.

Instructions regarding War Diaries and Intelligence Summaries are contained in F. S. Regs., Part II. and the Staff Manual respectively. Title pages will be prepared in manuscript.

WAR DIARY or ~~INTELLIGENCE SUMMARY.~~

(Erase heading not required.)

Place	Date	Hour	Summary of Events and Information	Remarks and references to Appendices
IN THE FIELD.	1.		Distribution of the Battalion as follows :- B Coy in the Left Sector with 2 Sections of A Coy. in support, under the command of Major MOORHOUSE. C Coy in the Right Sector with 2 Sections of A Coy. in support, under the command of Major MUNN. D Coy in Divisional Reserve at GODEWAERSVELDE. Advanced Battalion Headquarters at GODEWAERSVELDE. Rear Battalion Headquarters and transport at EECKE.	
	2.		The Left Sector heavily shelled during the day and night. Our Machine Guns fired 10,000 rds during the night on selected targets. In the early hours of the morning E.A. dropped bombs in the neighbourhood of HOOGENACKER.	
	3.		The whole of our front shelled at intervals during the day with H.E. and Gas shells, the vicinity of FONTAINE HOUCK receiving special attention. Our Machine Guns fired 15,000 rds on roads, tracks, etc. E.A. very active with bombs and Machine Gun fire. 1 O.R. Wounded.	
	4.		Our artillery very active in counter battery work. Enemy artillery normal in forward area but more active in the back areas. Our Machine Guns fired 15,000 rds during the day and night at E.A. and selected targets. 2 O.R. wounded.	
	5.		Artillery work on both sides normal. Our Machine Guns fired 12,000 rds during the day & night. 1 O.R. wounded.	
	6.		Persistent shelling throughout the day in the vicinity of IBEX Cottage, ST. JANS CAPPEL and FONTAINE HOUCK, including 40 - 8" shells. Our Machine Guns fired 4,000 rds. D Coy relieved B Coy in the Left Sector in accordance with Order No 30.	
	7.		Very quiet on both sides until 5 p.m. when FONTAINE HOUCK received attention. 300 H.E. & Gas shells of 8", 5.9., and 4.2. calibre falling. Our casualties were 3 men killed, 1 C.S.M. and 6 Privates wounded and gassed.	
	8.		Enemy guns normal except for a short period when he shelled the Quarry and Chateau on Mt. NOIR. Our Machine Guns fired 4,000 rds on selected targets. Enemy Machine Guns very active on roads and tracks during the night.	

Army Form C. 2118.

Instructions regarding War Diaries and Intelligence Summaries are contained in F. S. Regs., Part II. and the Staff Manual respectively. Title pages will be prepared in manuscript.

WAR DIARY
or
~~INTELLIGENCE SUMMARY~~.

(Erase heading not required.)

Place	Date	Hour	Summary of Events and Information	Remarks and references to Appendices
	9.		The enemy carried out harassing fire along the whole front with H.E.and Gas shells,sneezing and lachrymatory gas being used. A gas attack was carried out by us during which our Machine Guns co-operated,firing 5,000 rounds. Casualties - 1 man gassed.	
	10.		SCHAXTON & FONTAINE HOUCK received special attaention with 8",5.9's and 4.2's. Bewteen 12 m.n. and 12.30 a.m.the enemy carried out a gas bombardment on our front system.	
	11.		SCHAXTON & FONTAINE HOUCK were again heavily shelled. Our Machine Guns fired 9,000 rds during the night. Casualties - 1 man wounded.	
	12.		At 3.10 a.m.our artillery opened a heavy bombardment on the left of our positions. Enemy artillery much below normal. Our Machine Guns fired 3,000 rds on selected targets. During the night B Coy relieved C Coy in the Right Sector as laid down in Order No 31.	
	13.		Between 9 p.m.and 1 a.m.heavy gas concentration were fired on SCHAXTON and cross roads in R.34.b.	
	14.		The Quarry in M.26.b.,Mt.NOIR and our two left gun positions received attention during the day. Intermittent shelling of FONTAINE HOUCK and SCHAXTON throughout the day. Our Machine Guns fired 6,000 rds during the night. 2nd Lieut E.FORD wounded.	
	15.		The whole of our front intermittently shelled during the day and night with H.E.and gas. Our Machine Guns fired 14,000 rds during the night. Casualties - 1 man gassed.	
	16.		The usual harassing fire along the whole front. The Right Sector was subject to a heavy gas bombardment during the night. Casualties - 1 Officer and 18 O.R.gassed. Our Machine Guns fired 14,000 rds on roads and tracks during the night. E.A.dropped bombs on our front line at 10 p.m.	
	17.		During the day the enemy were unusually quiet except in the vicinity of IBEX Cottage. During the night our artillery carried out counter battery shoot and harassing fire,receiving a little retaliation. Our Machine Guns fired 10,000 rds during the night.	
	18.		Our artillery very active. Enemy very quiet. Our Machine Guns again fired 10,000 rds,receiving a little retaliation from enemy Machine Guns.	

A5834 Wt. W4973/M687 750,000 8/16 D. D. & L. Ltd. Forms/C.2118/13.

Instructions regarding War Diaries and Intelligence Summaries are contained in F. S. Regs., Part II. and the Staff Manual respectively. Title pages will be prepared in manuscript.

WAR DIARY
or
~~INTELLIGENCE SUMMARY.~~

(Erase heading not required.)

Army Form C. 2118.

Place	Date	Hour	Summary of Events and Information	Remarks and references to Appendices
	19.		Mt.NOIR,Croix de POPERINGHE and IBEX Cottage received special attention during the day and night. 5.9's,4.2's and 77.mm.being used. Our Machine Guns fired 12,000 rds on selected targets. Casualties - 2 O.R.wounded.	
	20.		Hostile artillery very active,NIRVANA Farm,SCHAEXKEN,Croix de POPERINGHE,St JANS CAPPEL,Stump Farm and WOLFHOUCK all being havily shelled. Our Machine Guns fired 13,000 rds during the night.	
	21.		Our support line intermittently shelled throughout the day. KOPJE Farm,SCHAEXKEN and St JANS CAPPEL shelled with 5.9's and 4.2's. Our Machine Guns fired 11,000 rds on selected targets and 40,000 rds in co-operation with the Division on our left as laid down in Order No 32. Casualties - 2 O.R.wounded. Lieut F.P.McCARTHY and 20 O.R.reinforcements joined from Base Depot.	
	22.		Enemy fairly quiet except during our bombardment. Our Machine Guns fired 11,000 rds on selected targets and 50,000 rds in connection with our Divisional operation in accordance with Order No 33 and 34. Casualties - 6 O.R.wounded, 1 O.R.Missing.	
	23.		Between 11 and 11.30 p.m.enemy put a heavy barrage down on our front and support lines. Our Machine Guns fired 20,000 rds in answer to S.O.S.call. Enemy Machine Guns fired short bursts over our positions in M.31.d.48.92.and along the road from Stump Farm to the White Chateau. Lt-Colonel G.de.HOGHTON, M.C.,proceeded to Base Depot.Major A.LOW, M.C.,assumed duties as C.O.	
	24.		Our old front line intermittently shelled throughout the day and night,Mt.NOIR and WOLFHOUCK also received attention . Our Machine Guns fired 4,000 rds during the night. Casualties - 1 man wounded. During the night C Coy relieved A Coy in the Left Sector in accordance with Order No 35.	
	25.		One of our Brigades carried out a local operation successfully. During the time this operation was in progress the enemy shelled our old front line and back areas,shooting very wild. Our Machine Guns fired 25,000 rds in co-operation with the Infantry attack. 15,000 rds were also fired on new S.O.S.lines on news being received that the enemy was massing his troops.	
	26.		Enemy very quiet except in St JANS CAPPEL area. Some gas shells were used.	
	27.		A little shelling around SCHAEXKEN,otherwise very quiet. Our Machine Guns fired 3,000 rds on enemy dumps, etc.	

A5834 Wt. W4973/M687 750,000 8/16 D. D. & L. Ltd. Forms/C.2118/13.

Army Form C. 2118.

Instructions regarding War Diaries and Intelligence Summaries are contained in F. S. Regs., Part II. and the Staff Manual respectively. Title pages will be prepared in manuscript.

WAR DIARY
or
~~INTELLIGENCE SUMMARY.~~

(Erase heading not required.)

Place	Date	Hour	Summary of Events and Information	Remarks and references to Appendices
	28.		Enemy artillery very active, the area round MARCHE CORSE was shelled for about an hour. St JANS CAPPEL was intermittently shelled with 5.9's throughout the day. From 7 to 9 p.m. gas shells were also used. From 10 to 11 P.M. salvos of 6 H.V. gas shells fell in the area round advanced Battalion Headquarters. The shells were all fitted with delay action fuses and penetrated to a considerable depth, the explosion could hardly be heard. Our Machine Guns fired 5,000 rds on BALLIEUL Asylum and vicinity.	
			Lt-Colonel J. MULLER, M.C., arrived to take over command of the Battalion. 2nd Lt C.G. BECKETT and 10 O.R. reinforcements joined from Base Depot.	
	29.		Area round IBEX Cottage heavily shelled with 5.9's. Front line intermittently shelled during the day with increased intensity between 6 and 8 p.m.	
	30.		German retirement from the St JANS CAPPEL Sector commenced.	
			2 p.m. - Letter received from Division stating that XVth Corps had patrols in BALLIEUL and BALLIEUL Station.	
			4 p.m. - Telephone message from G.S.O.1. cancelling relief by 35th Division and ordering Coys. back to the positions vacated by them the previous night.	
			4.30 p.m. - Orders issued to that effect - B Coy to Right Sector, C Coy to Left Sector, D " to FINNACE Cottage positions with 4 guns in Reserve. D Coy - 8 guns in reserve at GODEWAERSVELDE. A Coy - In Divisional Reserve,	
			Relief complete by 2.30 a.m. 31st August.	
	31.	8 a.m.	C.O. moved forward to advanced Div. Hd. Qrs., Mt. des. CATS.	
		11 am.	C Coy's fighting limbers ordered up to join ~~the other half coy. The whole coy in reserve to 107th Inf Bde at Mt KOKEREL~~ their Coy in the line.	
		~~2 p.m.~~ 11.30 a.m.	8 guns of D Coy ordered up to join the other half Coy. The whole Coy in Reserve to 107th Bde. at BUDGET CORSE.	
		2 p.m.	Rear Bn. Hd. Qrs. joined Adv. Bn. Hd. Qrs. at GODEWAERSVELDE.	
		4 p.m.	A Coy ordered forward to the MUELHOUCK.	
		6 p.m.	Adv. Bn. Hd. Qrs. moved forward to St JANS CAPPEL.	
		11 p.m.	Orders received from C.O. for A Coy. to move forward at dawn and to take up a defensive position on the RAVELSBURG Spur.	J. Muller ....Lt-Colonel. Comdg 36th Bn Machine Gun Corps.

A5834 Wt. W4973/M687 750,000 8/16 D. D. & L. Ltd. Forms/C.2118/13.

Army Form C. 2118.

WAR DIARY
or
~~INTELLIGENCE SUMMARY.~~
(Erase heading not required.)

36th Battalion Machine Gun Corps. September 1918.

Instructions regarding War Diaries and Intelligence Summaries are contained in F. S. Regs., Part II. and the Staff Manual respectively. Title pages will be prepared in manuscript.

982 8

Place	Date	Hour	Summary of Events and Information	Remarks and references to Appendices
On Service.	1.	4 a.m	'A'Coy moved out of St JANS CAPPEL for RAVELSBURG. During the day many large explosions occurred behind enemy lines. Innumerable fires burning throughout the day. 'B'Coy at dusk moved forward with 108th Brigade, passed through 109th Brigade and 36th Bn M.G.Corps and took up another line. 'C'Coy withdrew with 109th Brigade to BUDGET COPSE. 'D'Coy moved forward with 107th Brigade to an area around the Asylum in BALLIEUL. Major M.W.TAIT, M.C., joined Battalion and took over duties of Second in Command.	
	2.		Major A.LOW, M.C., left the Battalion and proceeded to 47th Bn Machine Gun Corps. 'D'Coy moved to the Asylum in BALLIEUL. Visual communication established, 25 messages transmitted. 'C'Coy detached from 109th Brigade and came in Divisional Reserve. 1 O.R.accidentally wounded (shot in leg with a revolver bullet)	
	3.		'B'Coy Hd.Qrs.moved forward with 108th Brigade. 'D'Coy moved forward with 107th Brigade. 'C'Coy rejoined 109th Brigade and moved forward at 8 p.m.to the Asylum, BALLIEUL. Capt D.WALKER reassumed command of 'C'Coy. Major E.V.WOOD,M.C., joined for duty and posted to command 'D'Coy,	
	4.		No change in the dispositions of Coys or Battalion Headquarters.	
	5.		Dispositions of Coys the same. Warning order received that the 36th Division would side slip to the left. 'A'Coy,36th Bn M.G.Corps will relieve the left Coy,31st Bn M.G.Corps. Our artillery very active along the whole front. Enemy's fire very moderate.	
	6.		The Division made a very successfull attack in which 1 Section of 'D'Coy took part, doing excellent work. 'C'Coy put a barrage down with 12 guns in conjunction with this attack. The enemy replied vigorously with his artillery. Casualties - 1 Officer(Lt HOPPER) killed. 1 Officer (Lt LEAVER)and 7 O.R.wounded. After the Officer Comdg the Section of 'D'Coywas killed, the Section Sergt.(Sergt CAPSTICK)carried on.showing great skill. For this deed he was awarded the D.C.M.	
	7.		Artillery on both sides very active. During the day the enemy confined his fire to the forward area but at night the back areas received a considerable amount of attention.	

D. D. & L., London, E.C.
(A8001) Wt. W1771/M2031 750,000 5/17 Sch. 52 Forms/C2118/14

Instructions regarding War Diaries and Intelligence Summaries are contained in F. S. Regs., Part II. and the Staff Manual respectively. Title pages will be prepared in manuscript.

WAR DIARY
or
~~INTELLIGENCE~~ SUMMARY.

(*Erase heading not required.*)

Army Form C. 2118.

Place	Date	Hour	Summary of Events and Information	Remarks and references to Appendices
On Service.	8.		Rather quieter during the day with increased activity during the night. During the night the Division side slipped to the left, 'A'Coy relieved the left Coy of the 31st Bn M.G.Corps.according to orders laid down in Order No 42. Casualties - 3 O.R.killed and 5 O.R.wounded.	
	9.		Enemy's artillery very active round Hill 63. Nothing unusual to report from other parts of the line. Casualties - 1 O.R.killed and 2 O.R.wounded.	
	10.		Very quiet all day. Our artillery carried out counter battery shoots during the night.	
	11.		During the early hours of the morning the enemy's artillery was very active along our front area. BALLIEUL, St.JANS CAPPEL and Mt.NOIR shelled during the night with H.V.shells. Casualties - 3 O.R.wounded.	
	12.		From 8 a.m.to midnight our artillery kept up a fairly continous fire on MESSINES Ridge. Enemy front line also continously shelled. The enemy's guns were active all day on battery positions and Plum Duff Street. From 10 p.m.to midnight HILL 63 and slopes of Hill about the Chateau were heavily shelled.	
	13.		During the afternoon and up to midnight our artillery fired consistently over the MESSINES Ridge. Enemy's front line systems were also periodically shelled. From 8 a.m. to 8 p.m. the enemy shelled our trenches in T.18.b.c & d.with 8",5.9's and 4.2's. The enemy's Machine Guns were active during the night around PLUS DOUVE Farm.	
	14.		During the early morning the enemy shelled our intermediate and back areas with H.V.shells. The NEUVE-EGLISE - MESSINES Road and batteries in vicinity were also shelled. About midnight a large number of H.E.and gas shells fell around L'ALOULETTE and our gun positions in T.11.d. Casualties - 3 O.R.wounded.	
	15.		The enemy shelled with increased activity during the day. Roads and trenches in T.18.b.and T.18.a.NEUVE EGLISE- WULVERGHEM Road,PLUM DUFF Street and batteries in rear receiving special ~~xxxx~~ attention from large calibre guns. Enemy's Machine Guns swept road in T.11.c.at intervals during the night.	

D. D. & L., London, E.C.
(A8001) Wt. W1771/M2031 750,000 5/17 Sch. 52 Forms/C2118/14

Instructions regarding War Diaries and Intelligence Summaries are contained in F. S. Regs., Part II. and the Staff Manual respectively. Title pages will be prepared in manuscript.

WAR DIARY
or
~~INTELLIGENCE SUMMARY.~~

(*Erase heading not required.*)

Army Form C. 2118.

Place	Date	Hour	Summary of Events and Information	Remarks and references to Appendices
On Service.	16.		We carried out a hurricane bombardment at 9.30 - 9.35 p.m.and 10.5.-10.10.p,m. The enemy heavily shelled areas in T.18.a.,T.18.b.,T.22.a.and T.22.d.during the day and night. During the night 'B'Coy relieved 'A'Coy in the Forward area as laid down in Order No 42.A.	
	17.		Very quite day. Nothing to report.	
	18.		Our artillery carried out a Counter Battery shoot to which the enemy retaliated vigorously with Shrapnel, H.E.and Gas shells.	
	19.		Between 9 a.m. and 11.30 a.m.about 50 enemy shells fell in T.22.a.and c. L'ALOULETTE,NEUVE EGLISE and roads in T.9.b.were all heavily shelled during the afternoon. The enemy's machine guns kept up a harassing fire from the direction of MESSINES on to PLUM DUFF Street during the night.	
	20.		Both sides carried out Counter Battery work,otherwise a very quiet day. During the night the 36th Division was relieved by the 30th Division in HILL 63 Sector. The relief of the 36th Bn M.G.C. by the 30th Bn M.G.C.was carried out in accordance with Order No 43. Battalion Headquarters and 'C' and 'D'Coys moved to GODEWAERSVELDE.	
	21.		'A' and 'B'Coys arrived in GODEWAERSVELDE about 2.30 a.m. The day was spent in cleaning guns, etc.and repacking limbers.	
	22.		During the morning Coys bathed At 7.30 p.m.the Battalion marched to the HOUTKERQUE area arriving about 11.30 p.m.and were accomodated in SHRINE Camp.	
	23.		The Battalion paraded at 10 a.m.to 10.30. a.m.for Battalion drill. The remainder of the morning Coys were at disposal of Coy Commanders.	
	24.		-do- -do- -do-	
	25.		-do- -do- -do-	
	26.		The Battalion was inspected by the G.O.C.36th Division and medals ribbons were presented to 2 Officers,3 Warrant Officers and 6 N.C.O's and men. At 9 p.m. the Battalion marched to ROAD Camp arriving about 10.30 p.m.	

D. D. & L., London, E.C.
(A8004) Wt. W1771/M2031 750,000 5/17 Sch. 52 Forms/C2118/14

Instructions regarding War Diaries and Intelligence Summaries are contained in F. S. Regs., Part II. and the Staff Manual respectively. Title pages will be prepared in manuscript.

WAR DIARY
or
~~INTELLIGENCE SUMMARY.~~

(Erase heading not required.)

Army Form C. 2118.

Place	Date	Hour	Summary of Events and Information	Remarks and references to Appendices
On Service.	27.		The Battalion left ROAD Camp at 8 p.m.and marched to DIRTY BUCKET Camp arriving about 11.30p.m.	
	28.		Orders recieved for the Battalion to move to POTIJZE. Moved off at 1.30 p.m. Bivouacs at POTIJZE Chateau. 'C'Coy moved with 109th Brigade to WESTHOEK.	
	29½.		Moved to dugouts at J.7.a.3.2.,800 yds West of WESTHOEK Cross Roads. 'D'Coy moved after 108th Brigade at 6 a.m. to POLYGON BUTT and on to BECELAERE.	
	30.		'C'Coy moved 2 Sectiosn on pack to TERHAND where they came into action. 'A'Coy attached to 107th Brigade and moved less 8 guns on pack to TERHAND arriving at 6 p.m. Very bad going. 4 animals bogged. Battalion Headquarters,B Coy,2 Sections A Coy and details of D Coy moved to vicinity BECELAERE arriving at 6 p.m. All transport reported at camp. Some casualties.	
			30th September 1918.	
			F.W. Jackson 9/14 Lt-Col. Comdg 36th Bn M.G.Corps.	

Identification Trace for use with Artillery Maps.

NOTE.—(1). These traces are intended to facilitate the communication of information as to the position of targets, which have been located on a squared map.

(2). The squares on this trace are 500 yards in length on the 1/10,000 scale, 1,000 yards in length on the 1/20,000 scale, and 2,000 yards in length on the 1/40,000 scale.

(3). The squares on the trace are fitted to the squares of the map showing the targets, which are then drawn on the trace. Sufficient letters and numbers must also be added to enable the recipient to place the trace in the correct position on his own map. A little detail may also be traced, but this is not essential. The name and scale of the map to which the trace refers must be always given. The trace can be used for the 1/10,000, 1/20,000, or 1/40,000 scale.

G.S.G.S. 3023.

Tracing taken from Sheet 28 SW 4

of the 1/10000 *map of* PLOEGSTEERT

Signature .... *Date* ....

SECRET. Copy No. 8....

No 36 Battalion Machine Gun Corps Order No 42.

---

1. Reference Operation Order No. 61, the 107th. Infantry Brigade is side slipping to-day, and taking over from the 31st. Division with boundaries as follows :-
(a) South. Hyde Park Corner - Red Lodge Road (exclusive) thence due Westwards from Red Lodge (inclusive).
(b) North. Messines - Gooseberry Farm - T.12.a.50.25. (Road inclusive) thence along Railway to T.1.a.10.10.
Brigade Headquarters will remain as at present.

2. O.C. "A" Coy. 36th Bn. M.G.C. after relief of the Left Coy. of 31st. Bn. M.G.C. to-day, will become O.C. Forward guns of 36th. Division.

3. "B" Coy. 36th Bn. M.G.C. will relieve "D" Coy. 36th Bn. M.G.C. to-morrow 9th inst., and on relief O.C. "B" Coy. will become O.C. Rear guns.

4. Guns will be sited in areas as shewn on the attached map, so as to cover the ground indicated by the arcs of fire also shewn on the map attached.

5. Special attention in siting guns will be given to approaches along the valley of the Douve, and through or South of Ploegsteert Wood, both of which movements would endanger the loss of Hill 63, which it is of vital importance for us to retain.

6. Arrangements for the relief og "D" Coy. by "B" Coy. will be made by Os.C. Coys. concerned, direct.

7. O.C. "A" Coy. will act as Group Commander, under the orders of G.O.C. 107th. Brigade.

8. Acknowledge.

[signature]............Capt. & Adjt.
36th Batt. Machine Gun Corps.

Issued at............p.m.
8th September 1918.

Copy No 1. Commanding Officer.
2. "A" Coy.
3. "B" "
4. "C" "
5. "D" "
6. 36th Division "G".
7. 107th Inf. Brigade.
8. War Diary.
9. " "
10. File.

S E C R E T.

Copy No..6....

36th Battalion Machine Gun Corps Order No 41.

1. The 36th Division is side slipping and taking over trenches now occupied by the 31st. Division.

2. "A" Coy. 36th. Battalion Machine Gun Corps will relieve the Left Coy. of the 31st Battalion Machine Gun Corps on 8th. September 1918.

3. O.C. "A" Coy. will arrange direct with Left Group Commander 31st. Battalion Machine Gun Corps to reconnoitre and relieve tomorrow, the Machine Gun Company in the Left Sector now held by 31st. Division.

4. O.C. "A" Coy. 36th Battalion Machine Gun Corps will arrange details of relief direct and report positions of guns taken over.

5. Acknowledge.

......................Capt. & Adjt.

Issued at..11.20...p.m. 36th Batt. Machine Gun Corps.
7th September 1918.

Copy No 1. Commanding Officer.
2. "A" Coy.
3. 36th Division "G".
4. 31st. Division "G".
5. 31st. Bn. M.G.C.
6. War Diary.
7. " "
8. File.

SECRET. Copy No. 14

No [illegible] Battalion Machine Gun Corps Order No 42.A

1. On the night 16th/17th September 1918, "[illegible]" Coy. will relieve "[illegible]" Coy. in the forward area of the line.

2. On relief "[illegible]" Coy. will occupy the positions vacated by "[illegible]" Coy. in the [illegible] line.

3. Not more than two sections of "[illegible]" Coy. will move forward at one time to relieve "[illegible]" Coy.
The remaining two sections will wait until the first half relief is completed before moving forward.

4. Further details of relief will be arranged by Company Commanders concerned.

5. O.C. "[illegible]" Coy. will remain Group Commander, and will be O.C. Rear Guns also.
O.C. "[illegible]" Coy. will be O.C. Forward Guns.

6. Lists of Trench Stores taken over will be rendered to Battn. Headquarters by 9 a.m. 17th September.

7. Relief complete will be reported by Code Words "[illegible]".

8. Acknowledge.

J. Wilson ....Capt. & Adjt.
[illegible] Batt. Machine Gun Corps.

Issued at ....p.m.
16th September 1918.

Copy No 1. Commanding Officer.
2. "[illegible]" Coy.
3. "[illegible]" "
4. "[illegible]" "
5. "[illegible]" "
6. Transport Officer.
7. Signal Officer.
8. [illegible] Division "[illegible]".
9. [illegible] Infantry Brigade.
10. [illegible] Batt. M.G.C.
11. [illegible] Batt. M.G.C.
12. War Diary.
13. " "
14. File.

Instructions regarding War Diaries and Intelligence Summaries are contained in F. S. Regs., Part II. and the Staff Manual respectively. Title pages will be prepared in manuscript.

WAR DIARY
or
INTELLIGENCE SUMMARY.
(Erase heading not required.)

36th Bn. M.G.C.

Army Form C. 2118.

Oct. 1918.

Vol 9

Place	Date	Hour	Summary of Events and Information	Remarks and references to Appendices
On Service.	Oct.		Reference HAZEBROUCK & TOURNAI 1/100,000. Sheets 28 & 29 1/40,000. 28 N.E. 29 N.W. 28 S.E. 29 S.W. 1/20,000.	
	1st.		During the early morning of 1st October the dispositions of the Battalion were as under. "A" and "D" Coys. were engaged in the DADIZEELE - TERHAND area. The remainder of the Battalion was in divisional reserve as under :- Battalion advanced H.Q. 28.K.19.b.7.d. " rear " YPRES. "A" Coy. less 3 Sections 28.K.15.a.9.1. " " 1 Section K.22.a.9.6. " " 2 Sections with advanced Battn. H.Q. "B" " 28.K.20.d.1.4. "C" " less 2 Sections TERHAND. " " 2 Sections Battn. H.Q. "D" " less 6 guns TERHAND with 108th Bde. " " 6 guns Battn. H.Q.	
			During the morning "B" Coy. was ordered up to support the attack of the 109th Bde., and moved to DADIZEELE. Sections were allotted to the Battalions of this Brigade, and supported the attack during the afternoon by firing into DADIZEELE. By night time the line had settled down, and guns were sited for defence, guns of "D" Coy. being withdrawn into divisional reserve, and their positions being taken over by "B" Coy. During the day "C" Coy. had concentrated and reorganised at BECELAERE, and had reconnoitered positions for the defence of the BECELAERE ridge. "A" Coy. had sent up, also, the sections at Battn. H.Q. to the 107th Bde., and mounted them for defence in K.20.c.	
			Casualties 3 Killed and 2/Lt. HEMINGWAY and 20 O.R. wounded.	
	2nd.		Battalion Adv. H.Q. opened at KIRK FARM at 10.40. "C" Coy. was attached during the morning to 108th Bde., with orders to be held in readiness for an immediate move to defensive positions. At 17.00 the enemy launched a strong counter-attack against our positions on HILL 41 and succeeded in driving back the line for some distance. The line was subsequently restored.	

A5834 Wt. W4973/M687 750,000 8/16 D. D. & L. Ltd. Forms/C.2118/13.

[signature]

Instructions regarding War Diaries and Intelligence Summaries are contained in F. S. Regs., Part II. and the Staff Manual respectively. Title pages will be prepared in manuscript.

WAR DIARY
or
INTELLIGENCE SUMMARY.
(Erase heading not required.)

Army Form C. 2118.

Place	Date	Hour	Summary of Events and Information	Remarks and references to Appendices
	2nd.		During this counter-attack one section of "B" Coy. came into action against the advancing enemy and materially supported the defence. For this work on this occasion:- 2/Lt. A.A.ANGLE and 2/Lt. T.G.BECKETT received the Military Cross, and No. 133181 Pte. A.JEFFRIES the Military Medal. Guns of "A" Coy. on the 107th Bde. front obtained direct targets which they engaged. During the day and night indirect fire was directed intermittently against enemy centres of resistance in K.19.a and b. Casualties 13 wounded.	
	3rd.		During the daytime of the 3rd nothing of importance occured. WINDY CROSS ROADS and the area about them were engaged with indirect fire during the night. Casualties 1 Missing.	
	4th.		On the 4th the 1st Motor Machine Gun Battery was attached to the Battalion and mounted its guns for the Anti-Aircraft defence of Divisional H.Q. on the BECELAERE RIDGE with orders to be ready to move forward at 20 minutes notice. This battery subsequently withdrew to PROVEN. During the night of the 4th/5th PARK FARM BUILDINGS, and the area at L.19.d. were engaged with indirect fire. 2/Lt. W.H.BAKER joined the Battn. Casualties 3 wounded and 1 wounded at duty.	
	5th.		The 35th Battn. M.G.C. relieved "A" Coy. 36th Battn. M.G.C. at TERHAND. "A" Coy. returned to billets at K.13.d.2.5. "C" Coy. relieved "B" Coy. at DADIZEELE K.17.b. "B" Coy. withdrawing to divisional reserve at J.12.d.7.7. 2 O.R. joined the Battalion this day.	
	6th.		"B" Coy. 104th Battn., with lorry transport (6 3-ton lorries) was attached to this Battn. The guns of this Coy. were withdrawn from positions on the 9th Divisional front by limbers of the 36th Battn. 7 O.R. joined the Battalion.	
	7th.		"A" "B" and "D" Companies moved to the REUTEL area J.11.d. Division issued Warning Order No. 139 that the II Corps with the XIX Corps on right, and Belgian Army on left will resume advance on J. day (to be notified later).	

A5834 Wt. W4973/M687 750,000 8/16 D. D. & L. Ltd. Forms/C.2118/13.

Army Form C. 2118.

Instructions regarding War Diaries and Intelligence Summaries are contained in F. S. Regs., Part II. and the Staff Manual respectively. Title pages will be prepared in manuscript.

WAR DIARY
or
INTELLIGENCE SUMMARY.
(Erase heading not required.)

Place	Date	Hour	Summary of Events and Information	Remarks and references to Appendices
	7th.		11 O.R. joined the Battalion.	
	8th.		Battn. H.Q. and the details of "C" Coy. not in the line moved to REUTEL area J.11.d. Battn. Warning Order issued that the Div. would attack with the 35th Div. on right and 29th Div. on left would attack on "J" day. 25 O.R. joined the Battn.	
	9th.		"C" Coy. was relieved on night 9th-10th by "B" Coy. 104th Battn. "C" Coy. on coming out of the line bivouaced in the REUTEL area. While Battn. was at REUTEL defences against aircraft were arranged. "B" Coy. 104th Battn. mounting 4 guns at TERHAND and "D" Coy. 4 guns at BECELAERE. Casualties 1 O.R. wounded.	
	10th-13th. 14th.		From 10th-13th the Battn. remained at REUTEL resting, refitting and preparing for action. During this period "B" Coy. 104th Battn. was in the line with the 108th Bde. On the night of 13th "A" and "B" Coys. moved up with the 107th and 109th Bdes. which attacked on the right and left respectively at 05.35 14th, in the direction of KEZELBERG, MOORSEELE, GULLEGHEM and HEULE. The advance reached just west of MOORSEELE on this day, but was here checked. Guns of both "A" and "B" Companies worked well forward in close support of the attack, and engaged targets with direct observation. During the morning of the 14th the 108th Bde., and "C" Coy. attached to it moved up to K.18.c.6.3. Battn. H.Q. and "D" Coy. moved to 28/D.23.17.30. Adv. Battn. H.Q. to Adv. Div. H.Q. at KIRK FARM. 15 O.R. joined the Battn. on the 10th. Casualties 3 killed, 18 wounded, 1 missing and Lt. Fox wounded at duty on 14th.	
	15th. 15th-16th. 16th.		The advance was resumed on the 15th. MOORSEELE, GULLEGHEM and HEULE were captured. "B" Coy. engaged enemy machine guns which were checking the advance and materially assisted the capture of HEULE by supporting fire. Battn. H.Q. moved to BAKEWELL FARM, DADIZEELE, and advanced Battn. H.Q. with advanced Div. H.Q. to ASHMORE FARM. During the night 15th-16th the 108th Bde. with "C" Coy. attached passed through "A" and "B" Coys. (which remained in position) and continued the advance on the 16th, reaching the line of the LYS. During the evening the 41st Div. relieved the 36th Div. and all companies were withdrawn and assembled at ROLLEGHEM CAPPELLE.	
	17th.		The 17th was spent in baths and internal reorganisation at ROLLEGHEM CAPPELLE.	

[signature] Major.

A5834 Wt. W4973/M687 750,000 8/16 D. D. & L. Ltd. Forms/C.2118/13.

Instructions regarding War Diaries and Intelligence Summaries are contained in F. S. Regs., Part II. and the Staff Manual respectively. Title pages will be prepared in manuscript.

WAR DIARY
or
INTELLIGENCE SUMMARY.

(Erase heading not required.)

Army Form C. 2118.

Place	Date	Hour	Summary of Events and Information	Remarks and references to Appendices
	18th		On the 18th the 107th Bde. relieved the 11 Belgian Regiment d'Infanterie north of HULSTE along the line of the LYS CANAL from PLATSBEEK. "D" Coy. was attached to this Bde., and relieved 24 guns of the Belgian forces, 16 guns being sited in defensive positions in depth behind the Canal. During the day the Battn. less "D" Coy. plus "B" Coy. 104th Battn. moved to billets in LENDELEDE, arriving 15.15.	
	19th		On the morning of the 19th the situation was as under:- "D" Coy. in the line with the 109th Bde. The Battn. less "D" Coy. plus "B" Coy. 104th Battn. in divisional reserve in LENDELEDE. In the evening about 19.00 "B" Coy. moved up to support the 109th Bde. in forcing the crossing of the LYS. Under cover of darkness during the night 19th-20th the LYS was crossed by ferry and pontoon, and a line was taken up running along the road from C.25.d.80.05. to C.22.a.8.7. "B" and "D" Coys. supported this attack, crossed the canal, and came into action on the east side of it.	
	20th		On the morning of the 20th the 107th and 109th Bdes. continued the advance at 06.00 pushing on to general line GAVERBEEK at 1.17.a.5.2. - I.11.b.9.0., thence to SPITAAL. "B" Coy. 104th Battn. was sent up to the junction of the LYS and ROULERS CANAL to protect the left flank which was left exposed as the troops on the left were not advancing, and left LENDELEDE at 06.00. "B" Coy. passed to command of the 107th Bde. at 05.00 to support this operation. The objective was reached. Casualties 2/Lt. BAKER and 1 O.R. killed, 14 O.R. wounded, 1 Missing, and 2/Lt. HUTT and 1 O.R. wounded at duty.	
	20th-21st		On the night 20th-21st the 108th Bde. relieved the 109th Bde. in the line. "D" Coy. remained in position for the defence of the line, and came under orders of the 108th Bde. "A" Coy. was attached to 108th Bde., who ordered one section to be attached to each of their battalions.	
	21st		At 07.30 on the 21st the 107th and 108th Bdes. advanced in the direction of KNOCK and EVANGELIEBOOM, and made some progress, reaching a line from the GAVERBEEK at I.11.d.8.9. thence through I.11.b., I.5.d. and b. C.29.c. and a., C.22.d. and a to DRIES. "A" and "B" Coys. engaged snipers and machine guns which were giving trouble. After "A" Coy. had passed through "D" Coy. during the morning "D" Coy. was withdrawn into divisional reserve, assembled and re-organised at R.11.d.7.6. when they were reported complete at 17.00. "B" Coy. 104th Battn. was withdrawn also into divisional reserve in the area about B.17., and maintained touch with the 109th Bde. Casualties 2 wounded.	

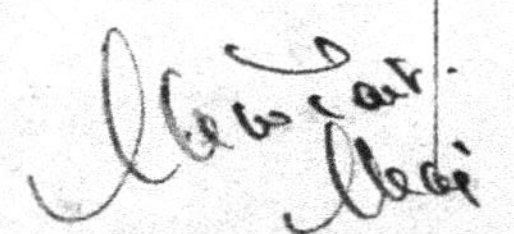

D. D. & L., London, E.C.
(A8004) Wt. W1771/M2031 750,000 5/17 Sch. 52 Forms/C2118/14

Army Form C. 2118.

WAR DIARY
or
INTELLIGENCE SUMMARY.
(Erase heading not required.)

Instructions regarding War Diaries and Intelligence Summaries are contained in F. S. Regs., Part II. and the Staff Manual respectively. Title pages will be prepared in manuscript.

Place	Date	Hour	Summary of Events and Information	Remarks and references to Appendices
	22nd		On the 22nd at 09.00 the line was advanced on the right to J.26.a.6.1., J.20.a.4.0., J.13.c.4.5., J.11.d.8.9. The division was constituted as a defensive flank, joining at DRIES with the French who had relieved the Belgians and whose line ran northward thence. "B" Coy. advanced with the Infantry. "A" Coy. guns were disposed for defence. During the night 22nd-23rd "C" Coy. relieved "B" Coy, in the line. "B" Coy. withdrew to ST. PIETER'S KNOCK. Here they returned to LENDELEDE in lorries and there reorganised. "B" Coy. 104th Battn. now transported by "B" Coy's. transport, was ordered to move along to an area on each side of the GAVERBEEK to protect the junction of the 107th and 108th Bdes., by disposing guns to a depth of about 3000 yards. Casualties 3 killed, 12 wounded, 1 wounded at duty, and 4 wounded (Gas).	
	23rd		On arrival at 108th Bde. H.Q. to make his reconnaisance O.C. "B" Coy. 104th Battn. learnt that the enemy was with-drawing, and the advance was to be resumed, and that, consequently, these defensive positions would not be required. The Coy. therefore, assembled in B.20.d. with H.Q. at B.20.d.1.9.	
	24th.		Battalion forward echelon moved forward to I.3.b. with Div. H.Q. Battalion rear moved forward to HULSTE area. "B" Coy. 104th Battn. relieved "A" Coy. 108th Bde. sector. "D" Coy. moved from ST. PIETER'S KNOCK to BEVEREN. Orders received from Div. for attack at 09.03 on the 25th in conjunction with the 9th Div. and the French. Casualties 1 killed.	
	25th.		Zero hour of attack altered from 08.00 to 09.05. Barrage lasting 3 minutes. "D" Coy warned to be ready to move forward with 107th Bde. Casualties 3 killed and 3 wounded.	
	26th.		Orders received for relief of this Battn. by 34th Battn. M.G.C. "A" and "D" Coys. moved to LENDELEDE Area under 107th Bde. Group. Bright day. "B" Coy. 104th Battn. remain under 34th Battn.M.G.C. Lt. R.Ahern and 66 O.R. joined this Battalion. Casualties O.R. 1 killed and 4 wounded.	

D. D. & L., London, E.C. (A8001) Wt. W1771/M2031 750,000 5/17 Sch. 52 Forms/C2118/14

Instructions regarding War Diaries and Intelligence Summaries are contained in F. S. Regs., Part II. and the Staff Manual respectively. Title pages will be prepared in manuscript.

WAR DIARY
or
INTELLIGENCE SUMMARY.
(Erase heading not required.)

Army Form C. 2118.

Place	Date	Hour	Summary of Events and Information	Remarks and references to Appendices
	27th.		"A" and "D" Coys. moved to new area, BELLEGHEM south of COURTRAI. Relief of "C" Coy. and "B" Coy. 104th Battn. "C" Coy. withdrew to LENDELEDE, and "B" Coy. 104th Battn. to ST. PIETER'S KNOCK, where their transport was returned to them, and "B" Coy's. transport sent to rejoin its Coy. at LENDELEDE on the 28th. Relief complete 23.40. Bright day. Hostile artillery active at night.	
	28th.		Command passed to 34th Div. at 12 noon. "B" and "C" Coys. moved to new area with 108th and the 109th Bdes.	
	29th. 30th- 31st.		Battn. less "A" and "D" Coys. moved to BELLEGHEM. The 30th and 31st were spent in refitting, bathing, inoculation, and general reorganisation in this area.	

D. D. & L., London, E.C.
(A8004) Wt. W1771/M2031 750,000 5/17 Sch. 52 Forms/C2118/14

36th Battalion Machine Gun Corps.

Army Form C. 2118.

Instructions regarding War Diaries and Intelligence Summaries are contained in F. S. Regs., Part II. and the Staff Manual respectively. Title pages will be prepared in manuscript.

WAR DIARY
or
INTELLIGENCE SUMMARY.
(Erase heading not required.)

November 1918.

Vol 10

Place	Date	Hour	Summary of Events and Information	Remarks and references to Appendices
On SERVICE.			Reference Maps. BELGIUM, TOURNAI 5. 1:100,000. Sheet 29) 1:40,000. Sheet 28)	
	1st.		The Battalion was in Corps Reserve at BELLEGHEM (29.N.27.)	
	2nd.		On the 2nd the Batta lion moved to the Rubber Factory, HALLUIN, and billeted in the German Barracks there.	
	3rd.		On the 3rd the Battalion moved to MOUSCRON, and were billeted in LE TUQUET, 29.S.20.21.	
	4th.		Training.	
	5th.		Inspected by the Inspector General of Machine Gun Units.	
	6th-12th.		Training of Personnel, Transport etc.	
	11th.		Armistice between Allies and Germans signed 11.00 hours.	
	13th.		The Battalion was inspected by G.O.C. Division.	
	14th-20th.		Training, Tactical Schemes, Recreations, etc.	
	20th.		Educational Classes were inaugurated on the 20th.	
	27th.		Sports were held on the 27th.	

J Muller.....Lieut-Colonel,
Commanding 36th Battalion Machine Gun Corps.

A5834 Wt. W4973/M687 750,000 8/16 D. D. & L. Ltd. Forms/C.2118/13.

Instructions regarding War Diaries and Intelligence Summaries are contained in F. S. Regs., Part II. and the Staff Manual respectively. Title pages will be prepared in manuscript.

WAR DIARY

~~INTELLIGENCE SUMMARY.~~

(*Erase heading not required.*)

Army Form C. 2118.

Vol 11

Place	Date	Hour	Summary of Events and Information	Remarks and references to Appendices
In the Field	Dec. 1918		Reference BELGIUM TOURNAI, 1:100,000.	
			On the 1st December the Battalion was at MOUSCRON, and remained there throughout the month, engaged in training, refitting, recreational training and education. On the 6th the whole division was inspected by the Divisional Commander at HALLUIN. On the 16th, also at HALLUIN, the Corps Commander inspected the Division, and said he was very pleased with its turnout.	
			An indoor Divisional Riding School was constructed by the Battalion, from the 18th to 20th, on the outskirts of TOURCOING. Cross Country Runs, and a Paper Chase formed part of the Battalion programme during the month; and tours were organised to BRUGES, OSTEND and ZEEBRUGGE, one by motor lorry on the 18th and 19th, and one by cycle from the 21st - 24th.	
			During the month 82 other ranks were despatched from the Battalion for dispersal as Miners and Demobilizers; 11 Miners and 1 Demobilizer on the 12th, 14 Miners on the 13th, 20 on the 14th, 5 on the 15th, 11 on the 16th, 15 on the 17th, and 3 and 2 on the 28th and 31st respectively.	
			Educational Classes were continued and new classes formed. By the end of the month there were 2 General Educational Classes, 6 French, 2 Mathematics, 1 Book-keeping, 1 Shorthand, 1 General Commercial Arithmetic, and 2 Carpentry Classes organised within the Battalion. In addition to these, men were attending a German class under Divisional arrangements, and a number of men had been sent to commercial, agricultural and engineering courses held under Army arrangements.	.... Lieut.-Colonel, Commanding 36th Battalion Machine Gun Corps.

(A7883) Wt. W809/M1672 750,000 4/17 Sch. 52a Forms/C/2118/14

Instructions regarding War Diaries and Intelligence Summaries are contained in F. S. Regs., Part II. and the Staff Manual respectively. Title pages will be prepared in manuscript.

WAR DIARY

or

~~INTELLIGENCE SUMMARY~~.

(*Erase heading not required.*)

Army Form C. 2118.

Place	Date	Hour	Summary of Events and Information	Remarks and references to Appendices
	1919. January.			98/12
In	1st.		Holiday. 20 O.R. demobilized.	
the	2nd.		Training, Recreation and Education. 4 O.R. demobilized.	
	3rd.		Battalion Cross Country Run.	
Field.	4th.		Interior Economy.	
	5th.		Church Parades. 2[illegible] O.R. demobilized.	
	6th.		Training, Recreation and Education 3 O.R. Demobilized.	
	7th.		" " " " 2 O.R. "	
	8th.		" " " " 1 O.R. "	
	9th.		" " " " 2 O.R. "	
	10th.		" " " "	
	11th.		" " " " 7 O.R. "	
	12th.		Church Parades. 1 Officer 3 O.R. "	
	13th.		Training, Recreation and Education. 12 O.R. "	
	14th.		" " " "	
	15th.		" " " "	
	16th.		" " " "	
	17th.		" " " "	
	18th.		Interior Economy.	
	19th.		Church Parades.	
	20th.		Training, Recreation and Education. 23 O.R. Demobilized.	
	21st.		" " " " 3 O.R. "	
	22nd.		" " " " 1 Off. 3 O.R. "	
	23rd.		" " " " One hour's Compulsory Education introduced.	
	24th.		" " " "	
	25th.		" " " " 1 O.R. Demobilized.	
	26th.		Church Parades. 4 O.R. "	
	27th.		Training, Recreation and Education. 3 O.R. "	
	28th.		" " " " 6 O.R. "	
	29th.		" " " " 1 O.R. "	
	30th.		" " " "	
	31st.		" " " " 1 Officer. Prince of Wales visited Unit with G.O.C. 36th Div.	

J. Muller Lieut-Colonel,
Commanding 36th Bn. Machine Gun Corps.

D. D. & L., London, E.C. (A8004) Wt W1771/M2031 750,000 5/17 Sch. 52 Forms/C2118/14

Army Form C. 2118.

Instructions regarding War Diaries and Intelligence Summaries are contained in F. S. Regs., Part II. and the Staff Manual respectively. Title pages will be prepared in manuscript.

WAR DIARY
or
~~INTELLIGENCE SUMMARY.~~

(Erase heading not required.)

Vol 13

Place	Date	Hour	Summary of Events and Information	Remarks and references to Appendices
~~In the Field~~. Mouscron.	1919 Feb.			
	1st.		7 Other Ranks demobilized.	
	2nd.		3 " " "	
	3rd.		12 " " "	
	6th.		2 Officers and 5 Other Ranks demobilized.	
	7th.		1 " " 4 " " "	
	8th.		3 " " 45 " " "	
	9th.		3 " " 53 " " "	
	10th.		1 " " 17 " " "	
	13th.		17 " " "	
	14th.		4 " " "	
	15th.		1 " " "	
	17th.		1 " " "	
	20th.		17 " " "	
	22nd.		1 " " "	
	23rd.		11 " " "	
	28th.		9 " " "	
			89 animals demobolized during the month	

.......[illegible]..........Lieut-Colonel,

Commanding 36th Battalion Machine Gun Corps.

A5834 Wt. W4973/M687 750,000 8/16 D. D. & L. Ltd. Forms/C.2118/13.

www.ingramcontent.com/pod-product-compliance
Lightning Source LLC
Chambersburg PA
CBHW081550160426
43191CB00011B/1884